A Sim[

Windows 98

G. Fouchard

Prentice Hall Europe

London New York Toronto Sydney Tokyo Singapore Madrid
Mexico City Munich Paris

First published in 1998 as Windows 98 – Se Former en 1 Jour by
Simon & Schuster Macmillan (France)
This edition published 1999 by
Prentice Hall Europe
Campus 400, Maylands Avenue
Hemel Hempstead
Hertfordshire, HP2 7EZ

A division of
Simon & Schuster International Group

Translated by Berlitz Translation Services UK, Baldock, Hertfordshire

Printed and bound in Great Britain by
Redwood Books, Trowbridge, Wiltshire

Library of Congress Cataloging-in-Publication Data

Available from the publisher

British Library Cataloguing in Publication Data

A catalogue record for this book is available from the British Library
ISBN 0-13-012195-9

1 2 3 4 5 03 02 01 00 99

Table of Contents

Introduction

This last version of Windows to be issued before the new millennium is strongly biased towards the Internet. In fact Windows 98 comes complete with all the navigation and communication tools required for the most effective use of the World Wide Web. But this system does not mark such a significant distinction as that between Windows 3.1 and Windows 95. The Windows 95 working platform is retained for users who wish to continue using it. However, the Web style of operating will be seized upon by those who wish to combine their PC operating methods with those of the Web facilities on offer.

Absolute beginners, or those who have just bought their first PC, do not need to know about the background history of the software. They will be able to catch up with the Internet and enjoy the full benefits of all the new system features.

In fact, Windows 98 has all the winning cards in terms of meeting consumer expectations; it contains all the features that made Windows 95 such a success and, as a bonus, it is scaled to the needs of the Internet. With Windows 98, computing is a real pleasure.

Each section in this book requires only one hour of your time to learn the various techniques: from mastering the basic skills through to delving into the most advanced features. In just one day you can discover this operating system, which will prepare you for the year 2000, and beyond.

ABOUT SIMPLE WINDOWS 98

This book is both:

- a **complete guide** to discovering the Windows 98 working platform and its tools and features, as well as the special features of individual software products, including Internet Explorer 4.0 and the e-mail manager Outlook Express;

- a **teaching method**, setting out the system features in twelve sections (one hour's instruction per section).

WHO IS THIS POCKET GUIDE DESIGNED FOR?

This very versatile book addresses a wide range of readers:

- **first-time users**. These will have just bought their first PC: they will enjoy the best of the technology available and will benefit from significant strides forward in the day-to-day use of a PC. Newcomers to the PC have an advantage over their predecessors who had to tolerate systems that were far less user-friendly.

- **Windows 3.1 users.** These will appreciate the simplified interface, the plug-and-play features and the virtual disappearance of DOS.

- **Windows 95 users.** These will discover how Windows 98 is integrated with the Web, plus an array of software for the Internet and more advanced system tools.

It will provide an essential aid to:

- discovering Windows 98 features;
- working or playing in Windows 98;
- linking you to the Internet;
- learning to surf the Web;
- using electronic mail;
- improving the performance of your PC and preventing faults; and
- gaining from the latest multimedia innovations.

ABOUT THE AUTHOR

Gilles Fouchard, an engineer by profession (Ecole centrale de Lille), is a software developer, an Oracle (database) consultant, an author and a magazine designer.

Since 1992 he has devoted his time to the launch and development of magazines: *Multimédia Solutions* (Edicorp), the first magazine in France devoted to multimedia technologies and then, in turn, *CD-ROM Magazine, Home PC, Internet Guide du Web* (Sepcom) and *PCmag Loisirs* (leisure pursuits).

Gilles Fouchard (**fouchard@planetepc.fr**) is the director of the Far Web company which specialises in the design, promotion and organization of Internet services for the corporate community.

Hour 1

The Windows 98 philosophy

THE CONTENTS FOR THIS HOUR

- A more user-friendly system
- A more reliable version
- A system plugged-in to the world at large
- A version that can be used by anyone
- An intuitive graphics interface
- Plug-and-play technology
- Playing a CD

Starting with the introduction of Windows 95, Microsoft has been simplifying the use of the PC on a day-to-day basis to win over new users and promote the system to all consumers. The major concepts developed for Windows 95 are reproduced in this latest operating system, Windows 98. We will go into these in more detail during the twelve hours of training set out in this book.

A MORE USER-FRIENDLY SYSTEM

It is no longer necessary for new computer users to learn about DOS (the *Disk Operating System*), because personal computing has moved on from DOS. However, applications operating in DOS can still be run: so you will be able to make the most of your old programs and especially all your favourite games.

A gateway to DOS
If you need to run a program in DOS, however, Windows 98 offers you a gateway that allows you to return to DOS. When you exit DOS, Windows 98 will be loaded back into the PC's memory in the same state as you left it when you quit. To open the DOS gateway, click on the Start button (in the bottom left of the screen), click on Shut Down and check the 'Restart in MS-DOS mode' option in the Windows 98 Shut Down window (see Figure 1.1).

Figure 1.1: Restarting the PC in MS-DOS mode

Compatibility with existing systems also includes recognition of the peripheral drivers and the network software. It was important that the system was able to accept the installation of a new item of equipment or peripheral (such as a printer or modem) quickly and easily. This new feature was based on a product strategy known as *Plug-and-Play*, implemented jointly by Microsoft and the leading players in the computer industry.

Whilst Windows 98 is compatible with the existing system with regard to certain matters, this is not the case in terms of performance. The idea of running Windows 98 on a 486 PC or even an entry-level Pentium processor is out of the question. In addition, memory (RAM) of 16 Mb is essential in order to run the system. For many existing users, the transition from Windows 3.1 to Windows 98 will call for a change of PC.

▬▬▬ The 32-bit architecture

The major technical advance, beginning with Windows 95, has been 32-bit architecture and better system resource management, which have created a more powerful, stable system. Windows 98 reproduces the 32-bit print manager and graphics manager technology that came with Windows 95. To this has been added the 32-bit model (the 32-bit Windows Driver Model – WDM 32) for peripheral drivers and the new file system in 32-bit mode.

The 32-bit file system
When beginning the installation of Windows 98 (see Hour 2), it is possible to request that your existing Windows and DOS files be retained in order to re-install them at a later date. You can uninstall Windows 98, provided you kept the default file management mode. Windows 98 is supplied with a system utility (FAT 32 converter) which allows you to change the file manager to 32-bit mode. If you make use of this facility you will not, then be able to change back to Windows 95.

Windows 3.1 users will also appreciate the multitasking mode of Windows 98, also a feature of Windows 95, which enables several applications to be run simultaneously. In Windows 98, 32-bit and 16-bit applications can run independently of each other. Each application is executed using its own disk space and does not affect any other applications.

The Windows 98 Registry

All technical information is stored centrally in a database known as the Registry. This database continually updates the PC configuration, thereby ensuring that Windows 98 operates at its best. It also has a role in the Plug-and-Play technology by establishing, each time an item of equipment is installed, which resources are unassigned (IRQ, I/O addresses, DMA channels, etc.) and allocating them elsewhere. Another advantage of the Registry is that it bypasses the notorious DOS configuration files AUTOEXEC.BAT and CONFIG.SYS, as well as the Windows 3.1 .INI files. Windows 95 users have already benefited from this new feature. The Registry can be looked up and modified from a remote location via a network, which is important for business users and DP managers.

A SYSTEM PLUGGED-IN TO THE WORLD AT LARGE

Under Windows 95, access to remote information servers was greatly enhanced. Access is gained in point-to-point mode or with specialised connection systems. As well as these connections, Windows 95 incorporated a centralised information send and receive system called Microsoft Exchange. This system, which supports the MAPI standard, provided a single location from which to retrieve fax messages or electronic mail. Although Microsoft Exchange still exists in Windows 98, it is somewhat redundant since e-mail traffic can now be handled by the Internet message system, Outlook Express.

In the space of the last three years, the Internet has made a major breakthrough, especially in home users, and the facility designed for Windows 95 no longer meets the needs generated by the phenomenal development of Internet communications. Windows 95 anticipated this development by adapting its basic architecture: it already incorporated a 32-bit version of the TCP/IP protocol (the communication and interchange protocol used on the World Wide Web). But making a successful Internet connection was a feat in itself. Since then, all resources possible have been deployed to integrate the connection process more effectively; the Internet Connection Wizard, supplied with the Internet Explorer 4.0 software package, now performs that function.

A VERSION THAT CAN BE USED BY ANYONE

For novices, Windows 98 brings its own clutch of new features and clears up a number of problems encountered in Windows 3.1. These significant changes bring the PC within the range of the greatest number of people ever and encourage its adoption by the home user. Here we should note that use of the PC differs greatly between business and domestic environments. Home users can now enjoy the benefits of the new generation of multimedia games, which rely increasingly on sophisticated synthesised animations. To this end, the new graphics display standards (*Accelerated Graphics Port* – AGP) are recognised by Windows 98. There is also the opportunity to enjoy easy, rapid Internet access and to use the Internet Explorer 4.0 navigation software to surf the Web, or to join in the discussion forums (*newsgroups*), not to mention the Outlook Express message system to send and receive electronic mail. Naturally, the PC running Windows 98, together with its electronic office software, remains an outstanding work tool. With the growth of part-time employment, teleworking and distance learning, the domestic PC bridges the traditional "business-home" gap.

Windows 98 incorporates all the key features that meet the requirements of the general public. It continues to use the features that made Windows 95 such a success and now incorporates the extra Internet dimension. With Windows 98, computing becomes a genuine pleasure. Here are a few aspects of the system to illustrate this point.

AN INTUITIVE GRAPHICS INTERFACE

The Windows 98 graphics interface is the same as that in Windows 95, which may take some time to get used to for those who have remained faithful to Windows 3.1 (goodbye to the File Manager and Program Manager). The Windows 98 interface offers a number of working methods – including the Web (see Hour 7) – and enables the user to customise his own environment. There is more than one way to execute most commands in Windows 98, as in Windows 95. To give one example, there are four ways of starting an application or opening a document.

- **Method one.** Hit the Start button to reveal a tree structure which shows the selected program or document (see Figure 1.2).

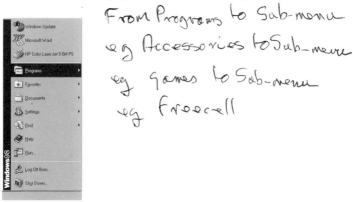

Figure 1.2: The Start button with its Programs and Documents sub-menus

- **Method two.** Select the program icon directly (provided you have found it on the Desktop first) and click the right mouse button to activate the Open command (see Figure 1.3).

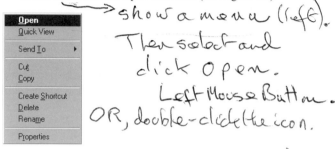

[handwritten annotations:] show a menu (left). Then select and click Open. Left Mouse Button. OR, double-click the icon.

Figure 1.3: The Open command

[handwritten annotations:] ✗ But it most already been the desktop

- **Method three.** Drag a program icon, for example, to the Start button; the application will then be entered on the main list under that button and you then simply click on it to execute the program (see Figure 1.4). *[handwritten: ✗]*

[handwritten annotation:] How is this different from Method 1?

Figure 1.4: The Aolsetup program has been added to the Start menu by a drag-and-drop action

- **Method four.** Create a shortcut that can be accessed on the Windows 98 Desktop. A shortcut is a quick link to an object (i.e. a program or a document) stored in the PC or accessible via the Internet. The shortcut is recognised by the little folding arrow that appears on the icon. To create a program shortcut, simply right-click on the program icon in question and select the Create Shortcut option (see Figure 1.5).

Must be similar to Method ...

See figure 1.3

Figure 1.5: The Create Shortcut command

This example illustrates Windows 98's ability to model its environment to suit your own needs. This option is ideal for use in a family context, since the PC can be adapted to children's tastes. In this way, the Desktop is enlivened with a background of images, icons can take on various shapes and, with the aid of sound, the Windows 98 Desktop takes on the air of a games arcade. Windows 98 provides a set of desktop user profiles, Microsoft Plus, which previously formed part of the Windows 95 add-on package.

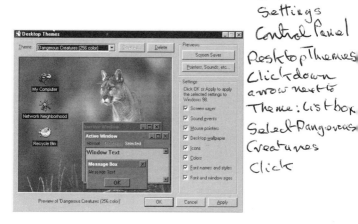

Figure 1.6: Choosing a profile from the Profiles icon on the Control Panel

The Windows 98 Desktop
The Desktop provides the main work screen. On starting up Windows 98, it includes the following items: the Start button, the Taskbar, a number of icons on the Desktop and an access area to what are called Web channels. The Taskbar is at the bottom of the screen, to the right of the Start button. The Desktop icons represent objects or shortcuts to objects. We will discuss these in greater detail later.

PLUG-AND-PLAY TECHNOLOGY

Whilst the success of the PC is due mainly to its open-ended flexibility, this is a setback for users who are nervous of installing a new item of equipment. With its new Plug-and-Play technology, Microsoft has imposed certain specifications on PC and peripheral equipment manufacturers. The aim of this has been to ensure total compatibility with the Windows operating system and to simplify, or even automate, the installation of memory and any add-on equipment. For this reason, Windows 98 is supplied with more than 1,000 drivers responsible for recognising over 1,000 different devices.

Plug-and-Play technology
The purpose of Plug-and-Play is to avoid conflicts such as interrupt handling (IRQ) or memory access management (DMA) by making the installation of equipment much simpler for the user. Plug-and-Play technology is based on three PC components: the BIOS on the motherboard, the controllers (ISA, EISA, PCI, PCMCIA, SCSI, etc.) and the operating system itself. The BIOS is a manufacturer's program which determines the hardware configuration of the PC. Each manufacturer must therefore make their BIOS compatible with Microsoft specifications. A Plug-and-Play BIOS sends Windows 98 all the information that might assist the end-user.

Windows 98 retains the Windows 95 Control Panel. This can be accessed by clicking on the Start button in the Settings menu.

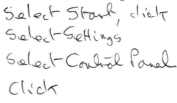

Figure 1.7: Access to the Control Panel

The Control Panel window contains an Add New Hardware icon which guides the user when installing new internal equipment (such as a graphics board) or external equipment (i.e. a printer, modem, etc.).

Figure 1.8: The Control Panel with the Add New Hardware icon

The Add New Hardware Wizard automatically recognises the new Plug-and-Play peripherals. If it fails to do so, you should select a hardware family and use a diskette to install the necessary driver. You can also download the driver from the manufacturer's Internet site.

Figure 1.9: The Wizard for installing new hardware with automatic detection of the hardware installed

Plug-and-Play technology

Plug-and-Play technology must satisfy a wide range of constraints. It is of vital importance that the hardware to be installed on a PC can be connected to the majority of known buses and connector types. These includes ISA, EISA, VESA Local Bus, PCI and USB buses, and PCMCIA, SCSI and IDE connections, as well as the monitor connections and the serial or parallel ports. This technology must guarantee automatic installation, loading into RAM and the unloading of drivers. It must also enable dynamic (hot) configuration changes which do not require Windows 98 to be shut down; this feature allows, for example, a PCMCIA board to be inserted without shutting down the machine. Finally, individual applications must be able to respond to these dynamic configuration changes.

Hour 2

Installing
Windows 98

THE CONTENTS FOR THIS HOUR

- Installing Windows 98
- On-line registration
- The PC Setup Wizard
- The benefits of the Windows Update program
- The new programs installed in Windows 98

Windows 98 can be installed directly on a PC:

- Without any operating system
- In Windows 3.1
- In Windows 95

Windows 98

16 Mb for Windows 98
First of all, check that you have at least 16 Mb of RAM – this is a prerequisite for installing Windows 98. The update for Windows 3.1 is likely to affect only a small number of PC users, since PCs supplied with 16 Mb of memory during the past three years will already have been equipped with Windows 95.

Insert your Windows 98 CD-ROM. In Windows 95, Autorun mode automatically starts up the Windows 98 CD-ROM, without the user needing to know the name of the start-up file.

The dialog box shown in Figure 2.1 asks whether you wish to upgrade your computer to Windows 98. Click Yes to reveal the Windows 98 Setup procedure.

Figure 2.1: The Windows 98 welcome screen

Figure 2.2: Windows 98 Setup

Click Continue. The Setup procedure will now check your system and then prepare the Windows 98 Setup Wizard to guide you through the rest of the process.

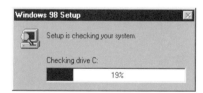

Figure 2.3: The configuration check

You may be be given a warning that you should close down all Windows programs before continuing. When you are done, click OK to continue Setup.

INSTALLING WINDOWS 98

The installation phases are as follows:

- preparing for installation;
- collecting information;
- copying files on the computer;
- rebooting the PC;
- hardware installation and final parameter set-up.

The procedure tells you what the average installation time will be (about thirty minutes in our particular case). This time is updated at each stage.

The Windows 98 Installation Wizard starts by checking the registry database and preparing the Windows directory from the beginning.

Uninstalling Windows 98
At the start of the installation phase, you can ask to save existing Windows and DOS files in order to re-install them later. You can then uninstall Windows 98. To do this you will need 50 Mb of hard disk space. Click Yes in the System Files window.

Installation steps to follow:

- **Acceptance of the licence agreement.** Click on Next to accept the terms.

- **Save system files.** Click Yes to allow you to uninstall Windows 98 and revert to your original environment.

- **Setting up Internet channels.** Select the country concerned ("France", for example) in the drop-down list.

- **Creating a start-up diskette.** This enables you to restart your PC if a problem occurs, or to run certain diagnostic routines.

When you come to the end of these initial steps, during the copying phase of your new operating system, you can learn about the major advances in, and new features of, Windows 98.

As you might expect, Windows 98 facilitates Web connections and recognises the various types of network you can use, especially the high bit-rate links such as ISDN. It includes numerous features, which will be described in detail throughout this book: it contains more multimedia and more games than Windows 95, and is also more user-friendly. Windows 98 is obviously designed for home use. Your office PC will seem lacking in comparison. Your new operating system will also be free of any year 2000 bug.

On completion of file copying, the Installation Wizard will reboot your computer. The Windows 98 Startup menu then offers you a choice of CD-ROM drive options (IDE, SCSI, etc.).

At this stage, preparing for the initial execution of Windows 98 may take a further 10 minutes or so. This stage includes building the peripheral database and the detection of Plug-and-Play components. The latter are installed and recognised correctly by the new system. Over 1,000 devices (modems, graphics boards, printers, etc.) are recognised by Windows 98.

The next stage involves installing the elements required for:

- the Control Panel;
- Start menu programs;
- the Windows Help facility;
- DOS program settings;
- setting the application start-up routine; and
- system configuration.

The system then reboots automatically, assembling the driver files required for machine operation.

Figure 2.4: The Windows 98 interactive display

On completion of the installation process, the user is presented with an interactive display showing:

- Register Now;

- Connect to the Internet;

- Discover Windows 98; and

- Maintain Your Computer.

Register Now

Click on 'Register Now' to acess the online Registration Wizard. After registering you will be notified of new products and updates and you can also obtain the best possible technical support. You will then be able to access the Windows Update program, the Web extension of Windows 98. This program will keep you up to the minute by:

- keeping your system updated, by downloading the latest drivers and system files; and by

- finding quick answers to technical questions you might like to ask.

The Registration Wizard will detect your modem and the communications port to which it is connected, unless you provide this information yourself.

The On-line Registration Wizard then lists details of your configuration. You can then send this list with your registration particulars. Click Yes and then click Next. Record the identification number of your product: you will be asked for this whenever you contact Microsoft.

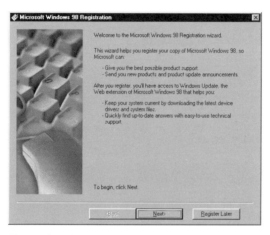

Figure 2.5: A step in the On-line Registration process

Discover Windows 98

This introduction is in four parts:

- Computer Essentials;
- Windows 98 Overview;
- What's New; and
- More Windows 98 Resources.

Start
Programs
Accessories
System Tools
Welcome to Windows
Discover Windows 98
Computer Essentials

Computer essentials is recommended for new users, who will find all the explanations required concerning the major operating features of Windows 98. For users with prior knowledge of Windows 95, this part is not necessary. For other users, it provides a useful refresher, which is ideal for going back over the chief basic principles such as the Taskbar, the Start menu, or even how the Desktop works.

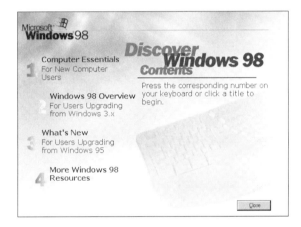

Figure 2.6: The Windows 98 interactive display

The Windows 98 overview includes a number of lessons on mastering the operating system. In six quick lessons, you will learn how to:

- starting a program;

- exploring files and folders;

- finding information;

- managing Windows;

- connecting to the Internet; and

- exploring the Active Desktop.

Information is provided at each stage: click on the Show Me button to display an animated presentation of a particular feature. This is a very practical way of visually memorising the commands to be entered.

▰▰▰▰ Maintaining your computer

Windows 98 invites you to set certain parameters to get optimum performance from your PC. You are offered two options:

- Express – Use the most common maintenance settings; or
- Custom – Select each maintenance setting myself. ~~myself~~ *yourself*

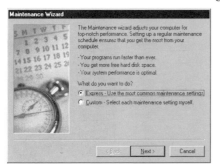

Figure 2.7: The Windows 98 Maintenance Wizard

When using the Express option you first define the time band for the Windows 98 automated settings. Choose from the three time bands offered – night, day or evening. Click Next and tick the checkbox 'When I click Finish, perform each scheduled task for the first time' to carry out these tasks immediately.

However, should you wish to alter the default settings of any of the scheduled tasks, double-click 'My Computer' and then 'Scheduled Tasks'. You can then access the settings for scheduled tasks as discussed below.

Disk defragmenter

Select Disk Defragmenter by double-clicking the icon. Under the Schedule tab you can define the interval between running the program, the date (e.g. every Friday at 9 p.m.) and the disk drive concerned.

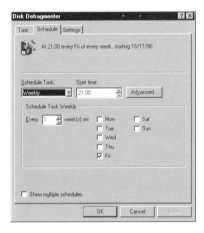

Figure 2.8: Scheduling disk defragmentation

Defragmenting a hard disk
This consists of retrieving vacant spaces and reorganising data files on your hard disk, so that the data in a particular file is contiguous rather than scattered around. The various additions, deletions and modifications you make in the course of your work cause the data in a file to be stored in areas that are not necessarily physically adjacent. As a result, reading a fragmented file becomes a much longer task. Defragmentation involves reorganising the disk space more rationally, thereby speeding up access.

Maintenance-ScanDisk

ScanDisk detects and corrects any errors in a disk drive. Select it by double-clicking its icon. You can now schedule this task and opt for a standard scan (checking files and folders) or a more thorough analysis. The latter also includes a test of the disk surface. This takes quite a long time and the system will ask you to run Scandisk if any problems arise.

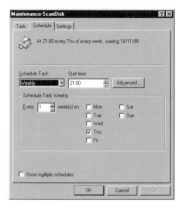

Figure 2.9: Selecting a disk-checking method with Scandisk

Maintenance-Disk cleanup

By double-clicking this icon and selecting the Schedule tab you can alter the settings (frequency and dates) for the program which clears out any any unwanted files, such as:

- temporary Internet files;
- downloaded files;
- old Scandisk files stored in the root directory;
- temporary files;

- temporary installation files;

- the contents of the Recycle Bin; or

- Windows 98 uninstall information.

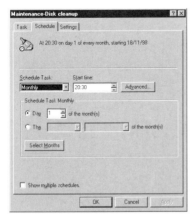

Figure 2.10: Dumping unwanted files

On completion of the set-up procedure, the Wizard provides a summary of the programmed sequences. Simply click on the Close button to confirm the selected options.

Connecting to the Internet

Hour 8 of this book is dedicated to connecting to the Internet. For now you should note that, on completion of the Windows 98 installation routine, a number of Internet programs will have been added to the Internet Explorer folder which can be accessed from the Programs menu in the Start procedure. These are:

- the Internet Explorer 4.0 navigator (see Hour 9);

- the mail and Outlook Express manager and the Address Book manager (see Hour 7);

- the NetMeeting communications software;
- the Internet Connection Wizard (see Hour 8);
- the Web page creation software, Frontpage Express; and
- the Web page publication tool, Personal Web Server.

We should add to this the system tools (the menu for this can be found by selecting the Accessories option in Programs), details of which will be given in Hour 11.

In the Programs menu, you will also find access to the NetShow multimedia software (see Hour 11) and access to the Kodak image-processing software, Imaging (see Hour 12). Note, too, the film management software, ActiveMovie (Multimedia sub-menu in Programs).

The Microsoft Windows 98 Web site
To learn more about Windows 98, you can find the Microsoft website at the following address:
http://www.microsoft.com/windows/windows98.

Hour 3

Discovering the interface

THE CONTENTS FOR THIS HOUR

- Your workbench: the Desktop
- My Computer properties
- The Taskbar
- The Start button.

Microsoft wanted not only to meet the needs of new PC users; it also aimed to offer solutions to problems encountered by more experienced users. The Program Manager, the File Manager and the Print Manager in Windows 3.1 were poorly designed; they have now been replaced by more consistent concepts and tools. Similarly, the Control Panel has been revised and improved. New concepts and a new working philosophy were good reasons for introducing a radically different presentation and operational procedure. Join our guided tour of the Windows 98 interface.

YOUR WORKBENCH: THE WINDOWS 98 DESKTOP

On completion of the PC start-up procedure in Windows 98, the workbench, or Desktop, is displayed. The system starts with the default presentation (or display) mode, which you can change later (see Hour 7) to Web mode. Various icons, distributed about the Desktop, give access to:

- Programs (the Internet Explorer navigator, and the Outlook Express message system);

- Folders (the on-line services offered on completion of the installation sequence);

- Shortcuts to documents

- Resources (My Computer); and

- Dedicated tools (such as the Recycle Bin).

This highly-organised Desktop facility conceals all the Windows 98 features and the application programs which might have been installed beforehand by the PC manufacturer, and all documents. Do not worry if you have just installed Windows 98 on top of Windows 3.1 or Windows 95: all your tools, programs, texts, images and multimedia files will still be there.

You can see three types of object here: the *icons*, the *Start* button (at the bottom left of your screen) and the *Taskbar* (along the bottom of your screen). One of the items shown on this bar (see Figure 3.1) is the Paint Shop Pro button, which is actually the program that was used to create the "screencapture" images in this book. The bar also features the My Computer and Online Services buttons, which represent the windows actually open on the Desktop.

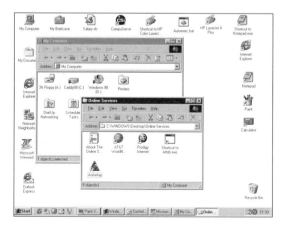

Figure 3.1: The Windows 98 Desktop, with two windows open (Online Services and My Computer)

This bar allows you to:

- use the Start button and run a program;

- open the window of a program waiting in the background (Paint Shop Pro, for example);

- to swap easily from one task to another (i.e. from one program to another, or from one window to another).

Taskbar and Switch To function
The Taskbar replaces the Switch To function of Windows 3.1. The new method offered is infinitely more practical. However, the Switch To facility can still be accessed by pressing the key combination Alt +Tab.

The My Computer icon provides an overview of your PC, which is more logical and easier to take on board than in earlier versions of Windows. A simple right-click produces a menu display – known as a context-sensitive menu – from which you can ask to open the My Computer window.

Figure 3.2: Opening an object (My Computer)

The My Computer window displays the hard disk drive and CD-ROM drive, the Control Panel folder, the printers, remote access to the network and Scheduled Tasks (Figure 3.3).

Figure 3.3: My Computer, a logical and global view of the PC

By double-clicking on [C:], you can open the contents of the hard disk. Each directory is represented by a folder and any files entered in the hard disk drive are shown.

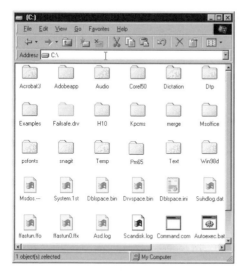

Figure 3.4: A logical view of the hard disk with its files and folders

MY COMPUTER PROPERTIES

In Windows 98, each object shown on the Desktop has properties
that can be easily looked up or modified. Simply highlight the object
in question with the mouse and right-click. This brings you to a
context-sensitive menu that enables you to open the object or activate
its properties. This operation allows you to look up the System
Properties. Here, four dialog boxes can be displayed successively
simply by clicking on the relevant dialog box tab: General dialog
box, Device Manager dialog box, Hardware Profiles dialog box and
Performance dialog box.

Figure 3.5: My Computer properties; Device Manager dialog box

- The Device Manager dialog box is used to examine the hardware configuration in precise detail. It is structured hierarchically: level one, or the root, represents the PC itself, whilst the second level brings together the major device families, shown according to hardware type.

The + sign to the left of each device (see Figure 3.5) means that the equipment in question may be detailed and comprises subsets. Hence, simply by clicking on the plus (+) sign, we can open out the tree structure. In the example below (see Figure 3.6) you can see a drop-down list of the System Devices. The list shows individual components, such as the PCI bus, the motherboard, and the memory access (DMA) controller.

36

Figure 3.6: Scrolling through the hardware tree structure, showing the list of system components

Inexperienced users need not concern themselves with all this technical information. This does, however, enable advanced users to examine their PC in meticulous detail and make any necessary changes. Double-clicking on any hardware component in the tree structure brings up a display of the technical characteristics of that component. The Properties button provides information on equipment operation, parameter assignments (settings), the resources deployed (in this case, the driver) and any hardware conflicts detected.

The hardware profile
The PC or computer you are working with is described by a hardware profile. On completion of the Windows 98 installation process, a default hardware profile is created, which collates all the technical characteristics of your machine. You can also create other profiles which can be activated at will when you start Windows. Whilst this facility is of limited use to the beginner, it can be implemented at corporate level when the same PC is used under different conditions, i.e. by more than one user.

Another dialog box (see Figure 3.7) provides information on the performance of your computer. From the basic information supplied, you can see the percentage of system resources used. Other advanced parameters relating to disk optimisation (File System button), Virtual Memory management or display optimisation (Graphics button) may be used by experienced users or corporate system administrators.

We will discuss object properties in more detail later. The example chosen here, although somewhat technical, shows how easy it is to obtain information on your working environment (in this case, the computer). At this stage, we shall confine ourselves to pointing out that the object properties procedure applies to all object families: an object can be the PC hard disk, a local area network, a program or a document.

Figure 3.7: The My Computer Performance dialog box

THE TASKBAR

The Taskbar is very important. It really serves as the control tower for your workbench. Its chief aim is to help you in your work and, as we have mentioned, to speed up the transition from one program to another or, to be more accurate, from one task to another.

This bar was designed to meet day-to-day requirements; in other words, starting an application, finding a document, passing from one task to the next, and so on. The Taskbar is split into parts with, from left to right:

- The Start button;
- The Quick Launch bar (see Hour 7);
- A list of active tasks; and
- A series of system settings icons.

Figure 3.8: The middle of the Taskbar displays the active resources; in this case, the screencapture program and the Outlook Express message system program

The right-hand side of the Taskbar contains icons which give access to volume control, display parameters, scheduled tasks (see Hour 11) and the date and time properties.

THE START BUTTON

The Start button is your real contact point in Windows 98. Simply click on the button to display a list giving access to programs and documents using Windows, or major commands such as the shutdown of the operating system. It can be set up and we have included in our example a CD-ROM menu that gives you easier access to your favourite CD library and the Internet.

Opening the Start menu from the keyboard
For convenience, when you are busy typing text at the keyboard and you do not want to use the mouse, you can activate the Start button by pressing the Ctrl+Esc key combination. Hit return to close the Start menu.

Figure 3.9: The Start menu

The small arrow to the right of certain menus means that there is a sub-menu for that option. Simply point to the selected menu with the mouse to display details. We have scrolled (see Figure 3.10) through the Programs, Accessories and Communications menus in turn.

With the Start button you no longer need to conduct time-consuming searches amongst different groups of programs. Nor is there any need to double-click on the icon of the program you wish to run (as you have to in Windows 3.1). The Start button gives you faster access to a program or document. It also does away with the "program" aspect of the Windows 3.1 interface since, from the Start button, the Documents menu gives direct access to the last documents used.

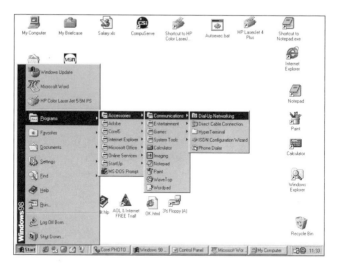

Figure 3.10: Direct access to a program using tree-structure lists; simply click on an object to open or execute it

The Programs menu

The Programs menu contains all the most frequently used applications. To run a program, simply select it in the menu and click. This list of programs and all other lists accessed from the Start button can be customised, as we shall soon discover.

Manipulating windows
When you run a program it opens an application window that you can close again by clicking on the X symbol at the top right corner of the window and you can expand it (maximise) or contract it (minimise) by clicking on the underscore symbol (_). When the window is minimised its icon can be seen on the Taskbar and you can restart it by clicking on it. This operating mode applies to any type of window.

The Documents menu

The Documents menu under the Start button lists the last 15 documents used and gives direct access to the My Documents folder. This again is very practical. A simple click brings back a document you recently worked on, irrespective of the program in which it was created. Remember that a document can be a text, a spreadsheet, a graphics image, a photograph, a sound file or even a video clip.

The Find menu

The Find menu under the Start button is used to trace a program or a file, to find a PC in a local area network, a document or service on the Web, or even to find individuals on the Net. The features offered here are considerably more powerful than those offered by the old File Manager, whilst their extension to the Internet greatly increases their usefulness.

Figure 3.11: The Find menu under the Start button

The Find all files or folders window (the equivalent of the directories in Windows 3.1 or DOS) offers three major options that can be accessed through dedicated dialog boxes. The first (see Figure 3.12) allows you to hunt for objects by name, from a given point in the My Computer tree structure. This is the Browse button which expands the tree and enables you to select an initial disk or folder.

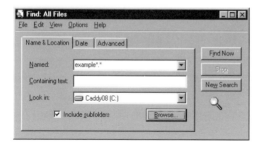

Figure 3.12: File search by name

This file search by name facility uses a character string that may contain the "wild card" characters '?' and '*'. Here are a few examples:

- Mode: find all objects containing the letters "mode".

- M?de: the '?' can replace any character.

- Mo*e: the '*' character can replace any string of characters between "Mo" and "e".

Figure 3.13 shows a typical search pattern, displaying details of the files found. The result may be displayed in one of four ways: by large icons, by small icons, by List or by Details. These options are available from the Display menu. _View ?_

Find by contents
The Containing text box enables you to conduct a search based on specific contents. Hence, in a set of signed documents, you can carry out your search based on the signature or key words of your choice. You can also find on your PC all the files that contain, for example, the words "Tourism in the UK".

Figure 3.13: The results of a search with display in Details mode

From the list found, the File menu offers a range of options. These options vary according to the nature of the object selected. Thus, in the case of a text file, the menu offers other alternatives, such as Print or Send To (see Figure 3.14). In the case of a folder, an Explorer option or a fresh search (Find, etc.) within the same folder is offered (see Figure 3.15).

Figure 3.14: The same File menu relating to a text file with, the Windows 98 Quick View feature

File Menu

Figure 3.15: The same File menu relating to a folder; here, the Explore feature

Windows 98 deploys the principles of dynamic processing depending on the properties of the objects you wish to find. Here, we pick up some of the options in the File menu, regardless of the type of object selected. Some options are common to all objects, whilst others are dependent on the type of object.

- **Open.** To open a document or start the selected program.

- **Open with.** When the nature of the selected object is not identified, Windows 98 sets out a list of programs that might be able to open the selected file.

- **Print.** A text file may be printed directly.

- **Play.** A sound file may be played immediately; to do this Windows 98 uses the Video Accessory, which is supplied as standard. At the same time, a video clip will be displayed in an independent play window.

- **Explorer.** A folder file is used to start up the Windows 98 Explorer. We will deal with this utility at a later stage (it replaces the Windows 3.1 File Manager).

- **Find.** If the selected object in the resultant list is a folder, it is possible to open a new search window that is identical to the last.

- **Send To.** This is a particularly powerful communications option, which we will also discuss in detail at a later stage. Three despatch options are offered: a fax addressee, a message addressee, or even a copy of the file on diskette. If your PC is equipped with a fax/modem facility, mail can be sent directly in this way. Instructions are given by the Compose New Fax Wizard.

- **Delete or Rename the selected object.** Deletion sends the object in question to the Recycle Bin, yet another new tool that we will describe in this section.

- **Properties.** Looks up the object's Properties.

- **Create Shortcut.** This option provides a quick method for accessing the object later.

A file can be found on the basis of its modification date: hence, you can search all files created or modified between two particular dates.

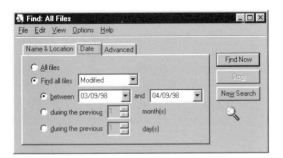

Figure 3.16: Searching by modification dates

FIND

Stop a search
The Stop button allows you to suspend processing at any time. This is useful if the processing seems to be taking too much time, especially if the file sought has just been added to the results list.

The Help menu

The Help menu under the Start button opens the Windows 98 Help facility. Online Help operates like hypertext language used on the Web: one click and you obtain links to another explanation, other programs or Wizards.

The Run menu

The Run menu is used to run a program directly when you know its name. If you cannot remember its name, press the Browse... button to search the Desktop or work from My Computer.

You will find that this command also allows you to open an Internet site or Web page address.

Shut Down

The Stop menu

You know how to start in Windows 98, but you also need to know how to shut it down. The Stop menu offers you a number of options:

Figure 3.17: Shutting down Windows 98

- total system shut down;

- shut down with immediate restart;

- shut down with restart in MS-DOS mode: a pointer allows you
  to reload Windows 98 in the PC's memory simply by typing
  "exit" at the DOS prompt (C:\ or any other directory).

Change of user on a PC
*The Disconnect sub-menu, which can be accessed from the
Start menu, closes down all active applications and opens
a new working session: if you choose this option, Windows
98 invites you to enter a new user name and password, so
connection is re-established under a different working
environment.*

Stopping a task without shutting down Windows 98
*Pressing the Ctrl+Alt+Del keys simultaneously in Windows
3.1 was irrevocable and forced you to restart the PC. In
Windows 98, the user can halt a current task in the same
way and carry out the necessary back-up procedures; these
are displayed in a dialog box.*

The Parameters menu

The Parameters menu comprises the following:

- Access to Taskbar and Start menu settings (see Figure 3.18).

- Folder Options management (see Hour 7).

- Active Desktop and Web channel management (see Hour 8).

- Control Panel activation (see Hour 4).

- Opening the Printers folder (see Hour 4).

- Updating Windows 98: this command starts the Windows
  Update program.

Figure 3.18: Windows 98 parameter settings

The Control Panel, which will be described later in this book, gives access to all the parameterisation features (Display, Modem, Joystick, etc.), plus the ability to add components (programs or peripherals). The Printers folder, also described below, enables you to set the parameters for a printer (either local, or accessed via a local area network) and to manage the transmission and reception of fax messages (by Microsoft Fax).

Taskbar settings

Finally, we shall examine parameterisation of the Taskbar. The first settings dialog box contains four options which you need to check or deactivate.

If the Always-on-top option is deactivated, the Taskbar may disappear or be partly obscured by a working window.

If the Auto-hide option is deactivated, the Taskbar disappears from the Windows 98 Desktop. It remains active, however: simply drag the mouse pointer to the bottom of the screen.

Figure 3.19: Taskbar settings options

to slowly bring it back into view. If you put the cursor back onto the Desktop, the Taskbar will drop down again and disappear.

You can also decide to display smaller icons under the Start button and to show the time on the right-hand side of the Taskbar.

Start menu settings

Even more important, you can customise the Start menu. The second dialog box in the Properties window for the Taskbar and the Start menu gives access to these features.

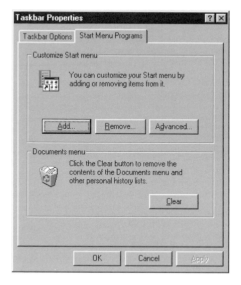

Figure 3.20: Choosing programs and objects in the Start menu

This settings dialog box is split into two parts: Customise Start menu and Documents menu. By clicking on the Clear button in the Documents menu, you can erase the list of the last documents used in Windows 98. As we have seen, this list can be accessed directly from the Start button.

To customise the Start menu, three buttons are available: Add, Remove and Advanced settings. In the next hour we will come back to these Customisation options.

Hour 4

Working in Windows 98

THE CONTENTS FOR THIS HOUR

- Changing from one task to another
- The Recycle Bin
- Starting a program
- The file management model
- Using the My Computer facility
- Handling files and folders
- File names
- Managing objects with Explorer
- The properties of objects

cont'd → pto!

- Shortcuts or methods for gaining quick access to objects

- Customising the Start button

- Handling diskettes

Working on a daily basis in Windows 98 requires familiarity with a certain number of operations (shortcuts) and tools (the Explorer), which will now be described.

CHANGING FROM ONE TASK TO ANOTHER

The Taskbar enables you to change easily from one task to another, from one program to another or from one document to another. The Windows 98 user is a true "screen hopper" with the ability to keep several jobs (windows) active simultaneously. It is the role of the Taskbar to ensure a smooth transition.

This bar, conventionally positioned at the bottom of the screen, can actually be relocated to any part of the screen. As various applications are activated, it shows all the buttons for the relevant active programs. These buttons are scaled down so that they can all fit on the Taskbar (see Figure 4.1).

Fig. 4.2

In our example Windows Explorer has been started first, followed by Microsoft Word, the Windows 98 audio CD Player utility, Microsoft Office and Windows 98 WordPad. WordPad and the audio CD Player are open and the CD Player is active. A MIDI music file is playing.

Figure 4.1: The Taskbar

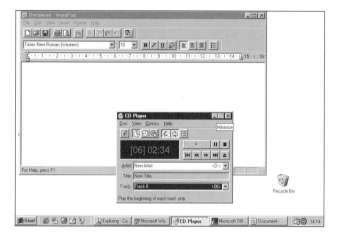

Figure 4.2: A view of the Desktop with two applications open, one of which is active

In Figure 4.3, the multimedia drive window has been minimised by clicking on the _ symbol at the top right corner of the window. The task remains active and you can listen to music at the same time as running the Windows 98 WordPad program.

Next, all the windows have been closed again by clicking on _ at the top right of the window (see Figure 4.4). To activate them again, click the relevant program button on the Taskbar. When a task is suspended like this, a very fast animated image shows the initial window being reduced until it takes the form of a button on the Taskbar.

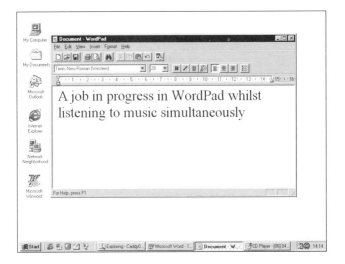

Figure 4.3: Another view of the Desktop with a job in progress in WordPad whilst simultaneously listening to music; all active tasks are indicated on the Taskbar

Conversely, reactivating a task restores the size of the button to the initial size of the working window.

The number of buttons on the Taskbar equals the number of active tasks, and buttons are automatically resized so that they all fit on the bar. For improved legibility, the user can increase the size of the Taskbar by dragging its upper edge with the mouse.

Finding out the properties of objects on the Taskbar
By clicking the right-hand button of the mouse on free areas of the Taskbar, you can call up the Properties of objects and adjust them accordingly.

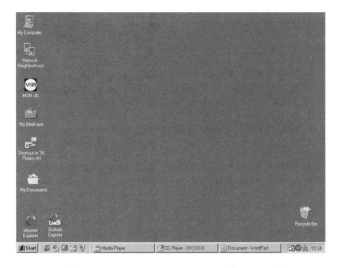

Figure 4.4: You can open the program of your choice from the Taskbar: in this case, the multimedia drive, the audio CD player or the WordPad word-processing application

THE RECYCLE BIN

The Windows 98 Recycle Bin is used to get rid of objects (folders, programs, text documents, images, etc.) of all kinds. In previous figures, the Recycle Bin is visible at the bottom right of the Desktop. To dump a file, simply click and drag the object in question to the Recycle Bin icon. Pressing the right-hand button also allows you to delete a selected object: it is then sent to the Recycle Bin. You can even select several objects at a time to delete by using the mouse and the Ctrl key.

NOT

Objects sent to the Recycle Bin are deleted immediately, however. If you make a mistake, you can open the Recycle Bin by double-clicking on its icon (see Figure 4.5). Point the mouse to the items you wish to retrieve and then press the right button (see Figure 4.6): the Restore option lets you correct the mistake. The Delete option is, however, irreversible unless you have a dedicated retrieval utility (undelete or unerase) on the disk. If you want to retrieve the entire contents of the Recycle Bin, you can activate the Restore option from the File menu. To empty the bin, use the Empty Recycle Bin option. If a confirm option has been set (it exists as a default), you will receive a final confirmation message.

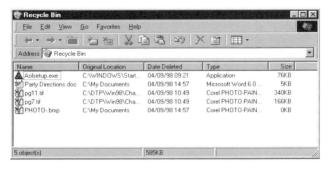

Figure 4.5: The contents of the Recycle Bin

Figure 4.6: Empty Recycle Bin irrevocably deletes the files from your hard disk

STARTING A PROGRAM

Several methods are available for starting a program that is not currently active. These methods show the versatility of Windows 98:

- From the Start button, select the Run command. *Enter program Name*

- From the Start button, select Programs and click on the program of your choice. This means that the program has been referred to previously in the Start menu; we will see later how to proceed.

- From the My Computer icon, scroll through the hard disk contents [C:] and when the pointer is positioned on the name (displayed in a list) or the icon of a particular program (displayed by icons), double-click to open the application. A further option is to click the right button of the mouse and select Open.

- The program could have been located earlier using the Find options, which are also offered in the Start menu.

- The Explorer program can be used to find an application and to run it.

- A shortcut may have been set up and placed on the Desktop. Double-clicking on the Shortcut icon also lets you start the program.

We can see from this example how the Desktop, My Computer and Start button menu provide resources for organising your work to suit your personal needs.

MY COMPUTER

In the My Computer menu (accessed from the Windows 98 Desktop), a disk or folder can be opened by double-clicking on it or, after selecting it with the right-hand button of the mouse, by activating the Open command. This calls up a window which displays the relevant files and folders as quite large, easily-readable default icons. Experienced users can reconfigure the display mode if they wish.

After opening My Computer by double-clicking on the icon, you can choose one of four display modes from the Display menu:

View

See Fig 4.7

- large icons;
- small icons;
- lists; or
- details (size of file, update time, etc.).

Figure 4.7: My Computer settings options; Folders display modes

We shall learn how to use the Explorer Bar, as Web Page and Folder Options commands, in Hour 7.

Handling files and folders

Files and folders can be handled very easily and moved around using the mouse. A right-click will enable you to Cut, Copy, Paste, Rename or Delete files.

Figure 4.8: File operations (context-sensitive menu)

The default display mode uses icons that are easier to read and easier to control than lists of files. This display method is also used in Windows 95. Lists will be appreciated more by advanced users, whilst icons are more likely to appeal to new users. An icon might, for example, represent a folder that can be opened by double-clicking on it, or by clicking the right-hand mouse button and selecting Open.

My computer, View, Toolbars, get-Menu

The View menu also lets you activate the toolbars: *Containing:-*

- **Standard buttons.** This bar gives access to basic functions (parent buttons to go up the tree structure, cut-and-paste functions, deleting an object, etc.).

- **Address bar.** This bar allows you to type in a file location on the hard disk or, as we shall see later, a Web address.

- **Links.** This option allows you to display a bar of links to Internet addresses.

- **Text Labels.** This option displays the standard buttons in compact mode.

File names
The limit on file names in Windows 3.1, where the length of a file name was restricted to eight characters plus a three-character extension, was a legacy of DOS. With Windows 98, as with Windows 95, you can use extended file names (up to 255 characters), without the need to type in an extension. The relevant extension for the file type is handled automatically by the program in which the file in question has been created.

MANAGING OBJECTS WITH EXPLORER

Windows 98 Explorer is the program in which to navigate folders and files, thus replacing the Windows 3.1 File Manager. Explorer provides an overall view of the PC's environment. All local disk resources (My Computer), as well as the disks that can be accessed via a network (Network Neighborhood) are displayed on the same level. This unique presentation greatly simplifies life for the user.

Windows 98 Explorer provides the user with an overall view of the objects and resources in the system, whether local or in a network. Explorer can also find documents on the Internet.

The Windows 98 Explorer can be called up in a number of ways:

- From the Start button menu: Explorer is listed under Programs;

- By clicking the right-hand mouse button on an object; in this case, My Computer (see Figure 4.9).

Figure 4.9: Using the right-hand button, you can activate the Explorer option; navigating begins with this object

The Windows 98 Explorer enables you to determine the contents of an object, whether this is My Computer , a hard disk or a folder. The left-hand pane of the window shows all the objects in the environment (this is the explorer pane), whilst the right-hand pane shows the contents of the object being explored.

Generally speaking, a folder contains files and other folders. It is possible, when using the detailed list display mode, to sort objects by name, by size, by type or even by modification dates (Modified). A second click on the same item reverses the sort direction. On the toolbar, five further icons can be accessed to the right: one of these icons enables you to display the Properties of an object, whilst the other four enable you to modify the type of display (Large icons, Small icons, List, Details). Depending on the nature of the objects examined, the detailed list does not necessarily show the same information: so by looking at My Computer, you can examine the total size of the disk drives and the space available on each of them.

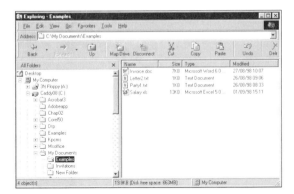

Figure 4.10: The contents of a folder in Explorer

Simply point the mouse to a free area to the right of the contents and click the right-hand button to create a new object (New command): a folder, a shortcut, or even a text file, WordPad document, Image or Sound. In this case, a new icon of the Image type appears in the window; you then simply give it a name. The object is created very easily, and double-clicking the mouse opens an empty document in Paint (the drawing program supplied as standard with Windows 98).

THE PROPERTIES OF OBJECTS

All objects handled in Windows 98 have properties that you can look up at any time, simply by right-clicking the mouse to activate the Properties command. You can find this feature in the Properties screen of My Computer. Several dialog boxes will be offered and you can change from one page to the next by clicking the relevant tabs.

If you want to look up the properties of the hard disk, the information supplied will, of course, be quite different. The space available on the disk in question is displayed in the General dialog box as a graphic (see Figure 4.11). The Tools menu offers three options:

- Scan disk to check it;
- A backup manager; and
- A disk defragmenter.

These three programs are part of the System Tools facility that can be found from the Start menu (see Hour 11).

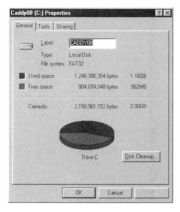

Figure 4.11: Displaying the Properties requested for the hard disk which were the amount of free space on the disk

SHORTCUTS: THE FAST WAY TO FETCH AN OBJECT

Shortcuts are extremely powerful links which will enhance your productivity in Windows 98. You can create a shortcut to any type of object – a file, program, folder or even the hard disk. Even better, you can put the shortcut where you wish on the PC, even in a document. When you open a shortcut, the object it is pointing to is automatically activated. Shortcuts are displayed in the same way as any icon: they represent the image of the object they are pointing to; they are distinguished by a little folded arrow at the bottom left of the icon.

Organising your shortcuts properly
The shortcut concept allows you to place an application, a document or an object in several files without the need to copy them. For instance, when running a multimedia application you need to delve into a number of folders. Each time you want to open a document, you have to change directory. If you create shortcuts, you can put all the shortcuts in the same folder, whilst leaving the original items where they were. Since the shortcut is merely a pointer to data, it occupies only a tiny piece of memory (255 bytes).

We shall create a shortcut to the screencapture program Paint Shop Pro. This can be called up from the Start menu but, as we have several screencaptures to do, we need to access it from the Desktop. A search (Find) will enable us to find this program on the disk: the program, named PSP, is in the Paint Shop Pro folder which is stored in the Program Files folder of Windows 98. From Explorer, position the mouse on this object and then right-click. The drop-down menu that appears offers the Create Shortcut command (see Figure 4.12). The shortcut can then be placed anywhere by dragging it with the mouse: either on the Desktop or, as we shall see, in the Start menu.

The shortcut can be moved to the Desktop using the mouse, but also using the Desktop Shortcut option in the Send To context-sensitive menu.

Open
Explore
Find...
Backup
Sharing...
Format...
Paste
Create Shortcut
Properties

Figure 4.12: Creating a shortcut

Placing a shortcut in the Start menu
To do this, drag the shortcut icon to the Start button. The shortcut will then automatically position itself in the main menu under this button, from where you can then run the programs you use most often without having to worry about where to find them. To place the shortcut in a sub-menu of the Start button, simply drag it to the Start button and release the mouse button. Next you can drag it from this position to another, say, in the Programs menu.

Thus, shortcuts can be moved to any location: to the Desktop, the Start menu and also to the My Computer icon. It's up to you! The most-frequently used programs could be placed under the Start button along with key documents, whilst you could position the disk drives or shared network resources with, for example, current business on the Desktop.

CUSTOMISING THE START MENU

We will now go back to Settings (in the Start menu) and activate the Taskbar, followed by Start from Settings. The second settings tab (Start Menu Programs) allows you to add or delete a shortcut (see Figure 4.13). The Advanced… button opens the Start menu in Explorer. At this stage, you are able to completely re-organise this menu by means of cut-and-paste or add operations. You can also drag a Desktop object to the Start menu.

Figure 4.13: Selecting programs in the Start menu

New shortcuts can be created directly from the File menu, under the Create a Shortcut option. Existing shortcuts can be moved, copied or deleted in the Explorer window, or even placed in this window from the Desktop (drag and drop with the mouse).

HANDLING DISKETTES

The disk drive can be accessed from My Computer. If the drive is used frequently, you can create a shortcut on the Desktop to read a diskette quickly.

The diskette is opened by a double-click, or from the Open command in the context-sensitive menu. The context-sensitive menu also allows you to access the diskette formatting and copying commands.

Figure 4.14: Copying a diskette

Copying files
To copy a PC file to diskette, simply drag and drop it with the mouse. You can also use the context-sensitive menu on the file and use the Send To Diskette command. Similarly, you can drag and drop one or more files from the diskette to a folder in the PC.

Hour 5

The Control Panel

THE CONTENTS FOR THIS HOUR

- The Control Panel
- Accessibility set-up
- Monitor display settings
- Mouse set-up
- Joystick set-up
- Modem settings
- Date and time management
- Sound management
- Multimedia set-up

Cont'd pto

- Printers and fonts management

- Mail, fax and Post office management (Microsoft Mail)

- Creating a password

- Installing new applications

- Installing new peripherals.

The Control Panel

At installation, Windows 98 will have optimised your system and set parameters for the individual components but, from the Control Panel, you can look up settings, improve them and adapt them as your environment changes. Thus, you can change your password, modify your monitor display settings or even install a new modem. The Control Panel can be accessed from the Settings menu under the Start button.

Figure 5.1: The Windows 98 Control Panel

Most configuration options are accompanied by Wizards to assist you. Wizards can detect and install a new peripheral without the need for the user to do a great deal, thanks to Plug-and-Play technology.

ACCESSIBILITY SET-UP

These are ingenious settings that enable users to tailor Windows to their own particular working environment. This is especially useful for new users and also for users with any physical disability, as special settings have been created to suit special needs.

The Accessibility Properties window comprises five dialog boxes which are selected by clicking on their tabs. For all the settings proposed, the Apply button allows you to try out the individual setting, whilst the OK button validates it.

Keyboard set-up

The first dialog box enables you to set up the keyboard. It offers three setting modes:

- sticky keys;
- filter keys;
- toggle keys.

Figure 5.2: Accessibility settings

To activate one of these modes, simply check the Use... box, then click on the Settings button to specify the key settings.

Sticky key settings

The underlying principle of the sticky keys is simple. Since activating the Ctrl, Alt or Caps keys is not easy for people who have a physical handicap or difficulty using key combinations, it is possible to make those keys active until you press a key other than Ctrl, Alt and Caps. This process makes input easy for those who have problems pressing two keys at once.

The Filter keys setting overrides accidental or repeated keystrokes.

The Toggle key function instructs the PC to generate a high-pitched sound when one of the Caps Lock, Scroll Lock or Num Lock keys is activated, or a low-pitched sound when one of those keys is de-activated.

Sound and picture settings

Figure 5.3: Linking an image or text to a sound message

The second Accessibility dialog box (see Figure 5.3) is used to link an image or text to a sound message in Windows 98. This is an option that will be appreciated by the hard-of-hearing. Two features are offered. The first is that Windows 98 will show a flashing sign on the screen for each sound generated by the PC. The area that flashes can be designated by clicking on the Configure button. The second feature makes programs display written captions instead of making sounds. Check the ShowSounds use box to activate this option.

You can also adjust the monitor display and select colours or fonts that are easier to read. To do this, check the Use High Contrast box, then click the Configure button.

Mouse set-up
The Mouse Settings dialog box enables you to use the four cursor keys on the numerical keypad to move the mouse, to click or double-click and even to drag objects. The settings screen allows you to define a shortcut key to switch this function off and to adjust the pointer speed.

MONITOR DISPLAY SETTINGS

The first option consists in choosing the screen background for the Desktop (see Figure 5.4). You can pick a wallpaper in bitmap format (BMP) which is then applied to the Desktop. By clicking on the Browse button, you can find a BMP file on the hard disk and assign it to the Windows 98 screen background.

The second settings dialog box is used to set up a screensaver.

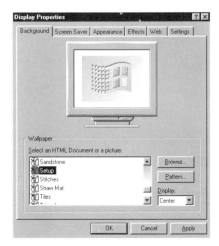

Figure 5.4: The Properties screen for changing Windows 98 wallpaper

> ### Testing screensaver mode
> *The selected screensaver can be viewed on the full screen by clicking on the Preview button. You can also protect your PC by means of a password. When your system is on standby, the animated screensaver starts, but your PC can only be used again by entering the password. The Wait counter indicates the desired period of inactivity before the screensaver becomes active.*

The Appearance dialog box (see Figure 5.5) enables you to set all interface colours (screen background, window title bar, control button, etc.) based on a given specimen.

Figure 5.5: Desktop appearance settings

The Display dialog box is used to adjust screen resolution and the colour box, provided the graphics board connected to the monitor accepts the selected values. The colour box can be set to 24-bit "true colour" mode (16.7 million colours), a mode used for processing photographs and bitmap images.

Web mode is used to set the positioning of Web channels (see Hour 8) on the Desktop.

MOUSE SET-UP

The mouse is so familiar to most users that it seems unnecessary to talk about it. Yet it does deserve some attention, particularly since once the mouse is set correctly, it can help your work in Windows 98. The first Properties dialog box (Buttons) is of interest for left-handed users (see Figure 5.6): once again, Windows will adapt to the user's preferences. Up to now, left-handed users have battled

away, using the left button of the mouse for selecting options and
the right button to obtain the context-sensitive menu (which allows
you to access the Properties of objects), but now you can change
the rules of the game. Simply click the Left-handed option in the
Button configuration menu.

Figure 5.6: Left-handed use of the mouse

From double to single-clicking
*The double-click action enables you to run a program or
open any type of object. You can bypass this by using the
right-hand button to display a context-sensitive menu. It
will be replaced – as we shall see later in this book – by a
single click if Web mode is used (to select a hypertext link).*

JOYSTICK SET-UP

Although, just a few years ago, joysticks were not very
sophisticated, today there are a number of models adapted to a
range of games software: flying a fighter plane, driving an F1 racing
car, etc. Broomstick, multi-axis spinners, multibutton controllers,

rudders – there are many variants of games devices. The Game Controllers screen (see Figure 5.7) enables you to select your equipment and set it up properly. It is simply not possible to indulge in aerial stunts without the correct broomstick settings.

Figure 5.7: Joystick set-up

MODEM SETTINGS

In Windows 98, everything has been done to help you communicate with the outside world. With a PC, all types of communication are possible, provided you have installed the modem correctly. If it is already present when Windows 98 is installed, it will in most cases be recognised and configured automatically. But you may need to enter new settings or switch from one device to another. The first dialog box (see Figure 5.8) allows you to look up the properties of the modem installed. The Diagnostics window indicates the connection port used and the More Info button is used to confirm that the equipment is working satisfactorily.

The second properties dialog box provides more technical information on the connection and dialling settings. The two buttons at the bottom of this dialog box also bring up the communications port settings and advanced connection set-ups.

Figure 5.8: A general description of the modem installed can be called up by pressing the Modems Properties button

DATE AND TIME MANAGEMENT

It is important that the date and time in your PC is set correctly. This enables you to program events (downloading on the Internet, PC monitoring) and to store your documents with the correct details (such as the date of last modification). You should also set the time zone by clicking directly on the map displayed, or selecting a region in the world from the drop-down list.

Setting the time
You can display the date and time properties by clicking directly on the time displayed on the right-hand side of the Taskbar.

Sound management

It is possible to link a sound to a Windows 98 event. Nearly 30 events (Windows start-up, Program error, Opening a window, Receiving new mail, etc.) can be set in this way for amusement or operational reasons. Hence you might link sounds to create battery run-down alerts for portables.

These sounds or audible messages are .WAV format files. If you have a sound board and a microphone, you can record your own messages with the Sound Recorder (Windows 98 Accessories).

Multimedia set-up

The Multimedia folder provides you with all the sound, music and video settings required. The Audio dialog box (see Figure 5.9) controls the sound board volume.

When Windows 98 is installed, the sound board fitted is automatically detected and is referenced as a peripheral by default. By checking the Show Volume Control box, you can alter the setting directly from the Taskbar.

Figure 5.9: PC audio settings

The same settings screen allows you to set the recording level for
those who have a microphone or other type of audio input device
and who wish to record files in WAV format on their hard disk. A
drop-down menu enables you to select the required quality: the
higher the quality, the larger the sound file will be. A number of
recording quality levels are offered and can be adjusted using the
cursor. The best quality offered is equivalent to that provided by
an audio CD.

The video settings offered are used to determine the size of the
video clip playback window. The options range from thumbnail
format ($^1/_{16}$ of the screen, through standard format ($^1/_4$ of the screen),
to full screen size. The full-screen format is acceptable only if you
have a graphics accelerator, or a suitable decompression board.

Figure 5.10: Setting the size of videos

The third multimedia dialog box is used to set MIDI parameters.
This is the standard for recording music files. As opposed to .WAV
files, which sample the audio signal, MIDI files are musical
commands associated with specific settings. You tell the sound
board and, in this case, the OPL2/OPL3 processor, which instrument
is to be played and under what conditions.

Listening to audio CDs on your PC
*If your CD-ROM drive incorporates a headphone socket,
you will be able, via the software, to set the volume level
for listening to audio CDs.*

PRINTER MANAGEMENT

The Printers folder is a shortcut which allows you call up printers
and fax settings, provided you have installed a fax board or module
in your PC. The folder is reached from My Computer.

Figure 5.11: The Printers folder

From here you can set up a printer or install a new one. By clicking
Add Printer, you activate the relevant Wizard. You can choose the
make and model and specify the connection port. You can decide
whether this printer is to be the software default printer. On
completion of the installation process, the Wizard invites you to
run a print test. This enables you to check that the printer is working
properly.

FONT MANAGEMENT

The Fonts folder gives access to all the typographical styles stored
in the PC. Here, the Fonts window shows the fonts recognised by
the system.

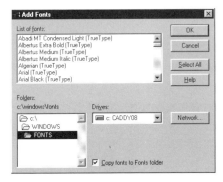

Figure 5.12: Adding one or more fonts

When you open a Fonts file, it gives you information on the font in
question and you can display the characters in different modes and
sizes. The Print button gives you a hard-copy sample of all the
possible variants based on that font (list of characters, character
size, etc.).

FAX AND MAIL MANAGEMENT

The settings for fax and mail management are directly related to
the Exchange program for Windows 98. This program uses a single
inbox to handle:

- fax messages;
- E-mail (Microsoft Mail); and
- Internet mail.

You need to install the components required for this inbox (see Figure 5.13), specify the modem to be used, any fax number, incoming call management and, for Internet mail, the mail-server details and E-mail name.

Figure 5.13: The Inbox Setup Wizard

POST OFFICE CONFIGURATION

The first time this facility is installed, the administration utility for a Microsoft workgroup post office is activated, which is a useful feature for companies. At this stage, you can administer an existing workgroup post office or create a new one by checking the appropriate option. The workgroup post office enables users connected to a local area network to receive E-mail (Microsoft Mail).

CONNECTION TO THE INTERNET

This icon in the Control Panel allows you to check your Internet connection and, if necessary, to modify its settings. You use the Internet connection Wizard to specify an initial (or new) connection to an access provider. The Wizard can be accessed from the Start menu or from the Connect dialog box (Connect button) in the Internet Properties window.

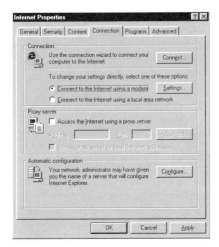

Figure 5.14: The Internet Properties dialog box

The other dialog boxes bring up different settings (see Hour 8).

CREATING A PASSWORD

Windows 98 and its various related services can provide protected access by means of a password (see Figure 5.15). You can change your passwords in the Passwords Properties dialog box. If your password was borrowed by someone else, or if someone has managed to obtain it through your own carelessness, you change it here. Use a little imagination if you really want to protect access to the system and make sure you remember your new password!

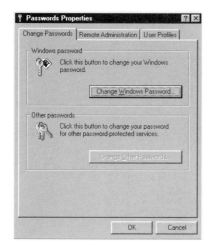

Figure 5.15: Changing passwords

Changing a password

To change a password, in this case the Windows 98 password, simply enter the old password, followed by the new one and confirm the new password. The same principle applies to all other services that may be available, such as connecting to a server via a local area network.

THE ADD APPLICATIONS WIZARD

From the Control Panel, you select the Add/Remove Programs icon and run the software install (or uninstall) routines from the diskette drive or a CD-ROM drive (see Figure 5.16). This utility searches the diskette or CD inserted in the PC for an installation program (of the setup.exe type) and starts the program it finds. To run it, click the Install button in the Install/Uninstall dialog box.

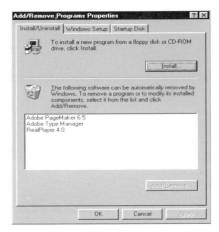

Figure 5.16: Installing a new program from a diskette or CD-ROM

Apart from installing applications, you can fine-tune the Windows 98 installation process by asking it to add a component not installed initially or remove a Windows 98 component. To do this, click on the Windows Setup tab. The program scans the PC to detect the resident programs. In the working window, you can select new components, or uninstall others.

THE ADD-HARDWARE WIZARD

Windows 98 also offers a guided procedure for installing any type of peripheral: CD-ROM drive, additional hard disk, display board, keyboard, modem, mouse, monitor, multifunction board, network adapter, PCMIA device, printer, SCSI controller, sound board, digitising board or joystick. This Wizard can also be called up from the Control Panel.

Figure 5.17: The Wizard for installing hardware on your PC

Hour 6

Windows 98 tools

THE CONTENTS FOR THIS HOUR

- The Calculator
- Notepad
- Word-processing in WordPad
- Paint drawing software
- The Phone dialler
- Dial-up networking
- Direct connection by cable
- The HyperTerminal utility

Windows 98 contains all the accessories that were included with Windows 95. These can be called up from the Start button by selecting Programs and then Accessories.

THE CALCULATOR

The Windows 98 calculator can operate in standard or scientific mode. To toggle from one to the other, simply select the type of calculator required in the Display menu.

NOTEPAD

Notepad provides a highly practical way of displaying a text file (see Figure 6.1) or entering text quickly.

Figure 6.1: The Windows Tips and Tricks file opened with Notepad

Date your activities in Notepad
You can create a dated log using Notepad. To do this, simply enter the command ".LOG" on the first line of the document, in the left-hand margin. Then save the file. When you call it up at a later stage, it opens with the current date and time at the end of the text. This enables you to keep a list of activity dates on a particular topic.

WORD-PROCESSING IN WORDPAD

If the Notepad facility does not meet your needs for inputting and editing text documents, you can use WordPad, a 32-bit word-processing program supplied as standard with Windows 98.

WordPad is an extremely powerful word-processing package, with a highly functional interface. Texts entered or retrieved in WordPad can be saved in the following formats (using the Save command in the File menu):

- Text only (.txt);

- RTF format, useful for exchanges with the Macintosh (.rtf);

- Word 6 for Windows format (.doc).

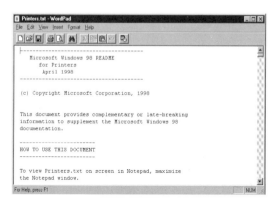

Figure 6.2: Word-processing in WordPad

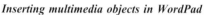

Inserting multimedia objects in WordPad
The Insert menu allows you to insert objects in a document. WordPad supports OLE 2.0 technology (Object Linking and Embedding) for incorporating objects. This enables you to use the functions of another application in WordPad and to create genuine multimedia documents.

PAINT DRAWING SOFTWARE

Windows 98 is supplied with Paint, a bitmap drawing software package that enables you to create customised background pictures for the Windows Desktop, or to prepare images to be inserted in WordPad documents.

From the File menu, you can ask for the image to be applied as wallpaper for the Windows 95 Desktop, either as:

- Default wallpaper (tile); or
- Default wallpaper (centred).

The Paint software incorporates a toolbox, a colour box and a status bar. These areas may be closed down from the Display menu. The toolbox offers all the conventional drawing functions.

Special effects
The Image menu allows you to work on the selected portion of the image. Hence, with Flip/Rotate you can rotate the selected zone horizontally, vertically or you can choose a particular angle. You can also invert colours: this gives you a negative of the image.

Figure 6.3: Customising the Desktop wallpaper using the Paint program

The Colors menu (see Figure 6.4) brings up the colour-handling functions. The Edit Colors menu enables you, from the basic colours, to define a set of customised colours. The palette you create can be saved and then used again later.

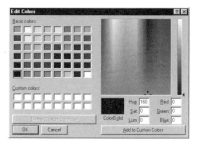

Figure 6.4: Defining customised colours

THE PHONE DIALLER

The phone dialler facility (Accessories, Communications) is used to set up telephone calls from your PC via the modem or any other telephone peripheral. The advantage of this lies in the ability to easily establish voice calls from your PC. To set up a call, you lift your handset and click Talk in the dialog box. To simplify your connections, the phone dialler facility incorporates eight memory locations (Speed Dial) for your most frequently used numbers. Simply click on each field to store details. A dialog box allows you to enter the name of a correspondent and their telephone number.

DIAL-UP NETWORKING

The dial-up networking function (Accessories, Communications) enables you to set up a connection to a computer or remote server. Once the call has been set up, you can access the network resources in the usual way. The only restrictions are those that might be imposed by the network manager.

A call is easily set up with the Make New Connection Wizard. First of all, you must give a name to the computer you called and select the calling modem. Then, you fill in the ringing settings, especially the line number of the remote server. When the settings have been confirmed, the Dial-up Networking folder will contain a new icon that provides the connection reference. This icon is used to establish the connection.

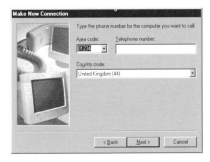

Figure 6.5: The remote server telephone number

Dial-up Networking is, of course, used to set up an Internet connection. For this, you use the Connection Wizard (see Hour 8).

DIRECT CONNECTION BY CABLE

The Direct Cable Connection (Accessories, Communications) transfers data between two PCs over a single serial or parallel cable. If you need to transfer data between a portable and a desktop machine, or between two PCs, this utility will be useful to you.

THE HYPERTERMINAL UTILITY

The HyperTerminal application (Accessories, Communications) connects you to remote sites or PCs by emulating a PC in terminal mode. In this way, your PC can be used as a terminal for a Unix machine, for example.

You need to define the connection step by step (for the initial connection): the name of server or PC to be called and related icon, plus server telephone number. You start the connection process and a dialogue is set up in the text window of the HyperTerminal utility. At this stage, you are recognised by the server and you must enter the *login* information (server name, user identifier, etc.). You can then send and receive files (using the Transfer menu).

Hour 7

Windows 98 and the Internet

THE CONTENTS FOR THIS HOUR

- The Start menu, and the Internet
- An enhanced Taskbar
- Different ways of working with Windows 98 Explorer
- Discovering Web style
- Links mode and the single click
- Different ways of working with folders
- Windows 98 folders settings
- Displaying reduced size graphics files

Windows 95 made it easier to use Windows 3.1 programs and introduced a document-oriented design philosophy. This philosophy has been continued in Windows 98. Windows 95 users can therefore switch to the new operating system without difficulty. Nevertheless, we shall spend the next hour describing the enhancements and extra features introduced in Windows 98, especially the integration of the Internet environment.

THE START BUTTON

Everything begins here in both Windows 95 and Windows 98. When you click on the Start button, you immediately find the user Log Off function. This is a useful feature for use in offices when a PC is shared amongst a number of people. At the end of a working session, you can log off without shutting down Windows. The next user can start the system using his own custom settings.

Figure 7.1: The user Log Off function

Calling up favourite Web sites

Figure 7.1 also shows you how to access your favourite Web sites. Click Favorites to call up your personal Web site organization. After installing Windows 98, you can find your preferred Web sites here (provided they were already selected in the browser). By default, four folders are offered:

- Recommended sites, generally determined in collaboration with your PC manufacturer.

- The Web channels offered by Microsoft, plus the worldwide channel guide.

- Technical links to the Microsoft site.

- Connection to the Microsoft site to update software such as the Web explorer.The Explorer 4.0 Update Channel web address is

  http://www.microsoft.com/ie_intl/ie40/download/cdf iechannl.htm

  and this is where you can register your copy of Internet Explorer at the Microsoft site. This gives you the benefit of future software updates.

No point, then, in starting up the browser first. It is quite normal to select a Web resource (URL address) first of all; the Internet Explorer browser will then start up automatically.

Figure 7.2: Calling up favourites from Start, Favorites

Finding documents on the Web

If you click on the Find option in the Start menu, you call up commands that did not exist in Windows 95:

- On the Internet
- People.

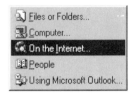

Figure 7.3: New search functions on the Internet, accessed from Start, Find

Figure 7.4: Searching the Web using the tools offered by Microsoft

Once you have logged on by double-clicking on Internet search, the navigator opens at the Microsoft site (**http://www.microsoft.com/surf/search/default.asp**). The Yahoo search engine is offered first, but you can switch directly to any of the following if you wish:

- Lycos
- Infoseek
- Excite
- AltaVista
- HotBot.

Start, Favorites
Search the Internet

Improve your search skills
The Web offers hundreds of search engines, directories, metasearchers and search tools. A difficult choice to make and, once selected, you still have to learn how to use the chosen tool. Each has its particular advantages and individual features. You would not use the same tool to look for a virtual travel agency, access a Web shop or even call up a software product.

Paging

Paging (searching for individuals) is conducted either off-line or on-line. You can look up a person's particulars in your Address Book (the one offered in the messaging software Outlook Express) or on the Web using the extensive search engines offered.

Searches in the Address Book are based on surname and forename, or just one of those. You can also base a search on an electronic address, a physical address or a telephone number.

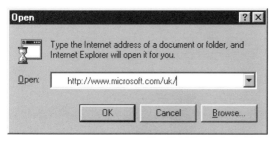

Figure 7.5: The paging window in the Address Book

There are paging directories and search engines on the Web such as FourII, Bigfoot, Infospace, Whowhere, Switchboard and Verisign. If you are looking for the electronic address of someone whose surname you know, these search engines can be of great benefit to you. Select a directory, enter the known information and click the Web Site button to start the search.

Executing a command

The Run option in the Start menu has a new feature in Windows 98. You can still fill in the name and path to a program you wish to run, but now you can enter a Web address (URL) directly.

Figure 7.6: Entering a Web address and logging-on directly

THE TASKBAR

Another new development – for Windows 95 users – concerns the
Taskbar, which shows four new icons to the left of the Start menu.

Right   Button

The Quick Launch bar

These icons perform the following functions (from left to right):

- Quick return to the Windows 98 desktop: one click on this
  icon automatically closes the windows of active applications.
  Those applications can still be called up from the Taskbar. You
  only need to click again on the same icon to go back to your
  original applications.

- Priority is given to channels selected via the navigator and these
  appear in full-screen mode.

- Starting the Internet Explorer 4.0 Web browser.

- Starting up the Outlook Express message communication
  facility.

*Figure 7.7: The four new icons on the Taskbar; this is
called the Quick Launch bar*

Adding new toolbars

Three other toolbars are pre-programmed and you have to activate
them from the Taskbar. These are:

- The **Address** toolbar, which is used to enter a Web address
  without the need to run the browser;

- The **Links** toolbar, which enables you access important Web
  sites without the need to open the browser;

• The **Desktop** toolbar, which arranges the shortcuts on your Desktop in a single location.

To display and use these toolbars:

1. Right-click on a free area of the Taskbar.

2. Select Toolbar.

3. Click on Address, Links or Desktop, as you wish.

Figure 7.8: Adding a toolbar to the Taskbar

Taskbar

Creating a customised toolbar

You will be able to enhance the Taskbar yourself by adding the tools that are most convenient for you. To do this, right-click on a free area of the Taskbar, select Toolbar and then click on New Toolbar. Enter a Web address or select a folder. The Web site or the contents of the folder can now be called up directly from the Taskbar.

Create a toolbar on the Desktop

If the toolbar is a bit crowded, or if it suits you better, you can create a toolbar on the Desktop from any folder. That folder may contain other folders, documents or Web addresses.

that is on the Task

This procedure is straightforward. Click a folder and then, keeping the mouse button pressed, drag it to the edge of the screen, as in our next example. Release the mouse button and the folder contents can then be accessed directly from a vertical bar.

Adjusting a customised toolbar
*The settings for this customised toolbar can be altered to
suit your needs. You can easily adjust its size by increasing
or decreasing its width. Just click on the edge and, as soon
as the cursor changes to a two-headed arrow, drag it left
or right as you wish. You can also move the bar away from
the edge of the screen. To do this, click on the top part of
the bar and, as soon as the cursor changes appearance,
bring the toolbar to the middle of the screen. Position it
and adjust its size as you wish.*

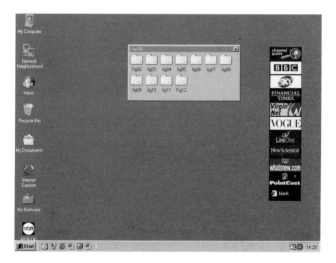

*Figure 7.9: The Working Documents toolbar has been
moved from the edge of the screen and placed on the
Windows 98 Desktop*

By right-clicking on a free area of the customised toolbar, you can
open the context-sensitive menu. This presents you with a number
of settings:

• Displaying objects as large (the default setting) or reduced size.

- The ability to hide the toolbar automatically. When the cursor drops below the edge of the screen, the toolbar pops up; as soon as the cursor moves away, the toolbar disappears. Only a vertical line (or a horizontal line, if the toolbar is positioned at the top or bottom of the screen) is visible when the bar is not open.

Hiding a toolbar
You can automatically hide a toolbar positioned at the edge of the screen; however, this feature does not work if the toolbar is positioned on the Desktop.

WINDOWS 98 EXPLORER

We will now look at some of the new features offered by Explorer. Due to the increasing popularity of the Internet, we now need to be able to work on objects stored on the hard disk and resident on Internet servers. Microsoft has thus adapted the Windows Explorer accordingly.

Figure 7.10: Windows Explorer. The As Web Page display is active, showing the contents of the Control Panel folder

Explorer runs the folder contents display windows: as the folders are scanned, you can call up the results pages using the Back and Forward buttons on the toolbar. With the Search, Favorites, History and Channels buttons, the Explorer acts like a browser. But the two tools remain distinct.

To start Windows 98 Explorer, click on Start, Programs and Explorer.

The Windows 98 Explorer components are as follows:

- **The toolbar.** With its new buttons: Back and Forward to scan pages, and Parent folder to go back through the tree structure.

- **The address bar.** To input a path on the hard disk or even an Internet address.

- **The left-hand pane of the Explorer bar.** With possible further expansions (the + sign means that there are contents to explore).

- **The results window.** To the right, in Web style in this case, with a Large icons display.

Windows 98 Explorer handles the folder contents display windows: as you browse, you can call up the results pages using the Back and Forward buttons. The toolbar also has a Properties button which gives you immediate access to the Properties window for the object selected. One click on the Display button (to the far right of the toolbar) takes you to the next Display mode (Large icons, Small icons, List and Details). As in Windows 95, you can call up this feature from the Display menu.

There is a new command in the File menu: Work off-line. In this case, you use Windows Explorer to browse your hard disk, as before.

Figure 7.11: The option to surf the Internet off-line (the File menu in Explorer)

The various browsing methods offered can be called up from the Display menu by selecting the Explorer bar. A number of options are offered:

- **Search.** Activate a search engine on the Web.

- **Favorites.** Open a list of folders containing your Internet favourites.

- **History.** Open a history file of past searches.

- **Channels.** Open the channels specified.

- **All folders.** This is the conventional system-wide exploring mode.

- **None.** This command shuts down the Explorer bar.

Surfing the Web with Explorer

To surf the Web, you are presented with the default search engines: Excite, Lycos, Infoseek, AltaVista, HotBot and Yahoo.

The search result is posted first of all in the explorer window (to the left). When you click on the addresses, the Web page shifts into the right-hand frame of the Explorer. Just point to an address to display the site on offer in the results part of the screen, on the right.

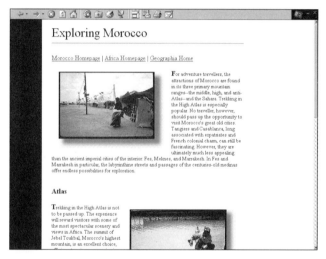

Exploring Morocco

Morocco Homepage | Africa Homepage | Geographia Home

For adventure travellers, the attractions of Morocco are found in its three primary mountain ranges—the middle, high, and anti-Atlas—and the Sahara. Trekking in the High Atlas is especially popular. No traveller, however, should pass up the opportunity to visit Morocco's great old cities. Tangiers and Casablanca, long associated with expatriates and French colonial charm, can still be fascinating. However, they are ultimately much less appealing than the ancient imperial cities of the interior: Fes, Meknes, and Marrakesh. In Fes and Marrakesh in particular, the labyrinthine streets and passages of the centuries-old medinas offer endless possibilities for exploration.

Atlas

Trekking in the High Atlas is not to be passed up. The experience will reward visitors with some of the most spectacular scenery and views in Africa. The summit of Jebel Toubkal, Morocco's highest mountain, is an excellent choice,

Figure 7.12: Switching to full-screen mode

Displaying a Web site in optimum conditions
Once you have found the site you want, you will find it easier to view the page in full-screen mode. Click on the Full screen icon on the Explorer toolbar. The Explorer pane vanishes and the page occupies the entire screen (see Figure 7.12). You can even hide the small toolbar temporarily: right-click on a free area of the bar and select Auto Hide.

Adding a page to Favorites

The Web page on Morocco (see Figure 7.12) can be added to your Favorites. An easy way to do this is to right-click on the page in question: a context-sensitive menu is displayed from which you can select Add Favorite.

At this stage, you have a range of options:

- Simply adding the page to Favorites;
- Adding the page and being notified as soon as the page is altered;
- Downloading the page (and any linked pages) and taking out a subscription to the site.

Figure 7.13: The Add Favorite setting with the options of notice of an update or taking out a subscription to the site by setting the page downloading parameters

Similar features are, of course, offered in the Internet Explorer browser facility (see Hour 6). These are the original features of the Internet Explorer browser which, for practical reasons, have been duplicated in Windows 98 Explorer. These two tools may well be merged in future. In this way, Microsoft could realise its ambition to standardize the way in which we work with documents, whether they are stored locally in a PC or are resident on an intranet or Internet server.

Arranging your favourite sites
When you add to the Favorites menu, your Web site is not placed in one of your Favorites folders. By default, it is placed in the Favorites root directory. If this is not what you want, you should re-arrange your Favorites: use the Arrange Favorites feature which you can call up from the Favorites menu, now included in Explorer.

Another way to do this is to click on the Favorites button, if you have not already done so; your favourite sites and folders are then listed in the Explorer pane; click on your new favourite at the bottom of the list and, keeping the mouse button pressed, drag it to your chosen folder.

Sending a Web page by e-mail

You have probably noticed that the enhanced Explorer toolbar contains a Mail icon. Apart from the proposed link to Outlook Express, this button allows you to send the site link (or the page itself) to another party. This is a very practical way of sharing your Internet discoveries with fellow Net users.

Figure 7.14: The Send Page by e-mail command (Explorer Mail button)

You might decide to send a page:

- **as an attachment.** The addressee can open it directly or store it on his PC hard disk.

- **in read-only mode.** In this case, it will be contained in the body of the message.

THE WINDOWS 98 DESKTOP IN WEB
STYLE

With Windows 98, you will discover new ways of working with
the Windows Desktop, especially Web style.This enables you to
browse through the folders on your PC in the same way as you
look up Web pages.

To switch to Web style:

1. Double-click the My Computer icon which is displayed on
   the Desktop.

2. Select the Display menu, followed by Folder Options.

3. Check the Web Style box in the General dialog box in the
   Folder Options window.

Figure 7.15: The Folder Options command

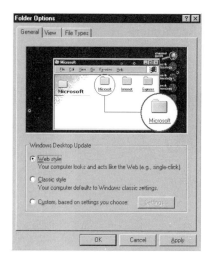

Figure 7.16: Select Web style to adapt your PC to Internet working methods

Classic operating style

If you want to go back to classic operating style, you can cancel Web style. To do this, bring up the Folder Options menu and slect Classic style.

An option entitled "Custom, based on settings you choose" enables you to tailor Windows 98 Desktop operation to your taste. Check this box and click on the Settings button: you can choose intermediate options between Web style and Classic style and keep the selected style by double-clicking it.

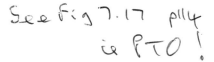

Figure 7.17: Windows 98 Desktop custom settings: single or double-click – the choice is yours

FOLDER SETTINGS

By using Windows 98 Web style, you can display and handle files in a totally different way. When you open a folder, it is displayed in a new and unfamiliar way. The folder name is clearly shown in the look-up window. Two further buttons indicate the option – if it is active – to switch from one window to another (Back and Forward). You can revert to classic operating mode by checking the second option, i.e.: Opening each folder in a separate window. This operating mode is far less practical because you multiply the number of working windows on the Desktop, but it can be useful.

Figure 7.18: The contents of a folder

Folder display settings

You may have noticed that the contents of folders are displayed as
Web pages. Each constituent object (whether it is a file or a folder)
is a link which you can open with a single click. You can do all
sorts of things with these Web pages and the Folder Display Wizard,
in particular, will help you in your task.

You may customise folders as follows:

1. Select the folder by pointing to it with the mouse (no need to
   click, it will open automatically). You will see that information
   about the folder appears on the left-hand side of the window
   (name, size of a file, date of last modification, etc.).

2. From the folder display window, activate the Display menu.

3. Select Customize this folder.

4. The Customization Wizard starts up.

Figure 7.19: The folder customisation command; note that the 'as Web page' option is active

Once the Customization Wizard is running, you are presented with three options:

- The first option is to create or modify an HTML document, which will allow you to alter the display of the selected folder.

- The second option displays a background graphic of the icons (objects belonging to the folder) that are contained in the folder.

- The third option returns you to the initial display.

Choose the second settings option and click the Next button. Find a graphic in .BMP format on the hard disk and select it as a folder background.

Display settings for all files

We have just discussed folder presentation and customisation methods. There is also a set of parameters which governs the display and the way in which we work with all the files resident in the PC. From the Start menu, click Settings, followed by Folder options. Next, select the Display option in the Folder options window.

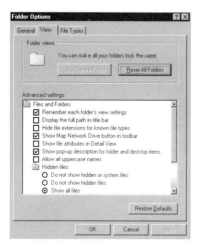

Figure 7.20: Folder display options

It is up to you to choose the files and folders options that suit your needs; you can also decide to display the file attributes in detailed mode, display hidden files or use layout settings such as font scaling. Use these options as you wish, but remember that the default settings are quite satisfactory most of the time.

Image file management

A major new feature in the Image file management facility allows you to view the contents of a file in Thumbnail Window form before you open it in a software package. This gives the folder manager an even more flexible interface, although it displays only one cameo (or thumbnail) at a time: i.e. the one to which the cursor is pointing. There is no need to click the button.

Figure 7.21: Displaying the selected file in reduced size

The My Computer folder

You can quickly obtain details about the hardware, especially about the free space on the hard disk. This procedure is easy: go back to the Desktop, click My Computer and point with the mouse at the disk drive [C:], but do not click. The total disk space and the space available are shown on the left-hand side of the display window.

Figure 7.22: My Computer: by pointing to the hard disk, you can obtain a graphic display of the total disk space and the free space

The best display mode

To bring this feature into play, you must select the 'as Web Page' option in the Display menu of My Computer.

Hour 8

Internet connection and Web channels

THE CONTENTS FOR THIS HOUR

- Logging on to the Internet
- Dial-up networking
- The Internet Connection Wizard
- Discovering Web channels
- How to take out a subscription to a channel
- Guide to on line channels

To log on to the Internet, your PC must incorporate a program that can handle interchanges with the network. Do not forget that so-called "personal" computers are designed to work independently and any connection to a network is based on the assumption that there is an interface. These add-ons may be supplied with the operating system in which case you just need to install them. This is the case with Windows 98.

When you access the Internet, the connection (log-on) program performs the following tasks:

- it sets up the link to the site of your Internet access provider (IAP); and

- it handles the data interchange protocol used on the Internet.

THE INTERNET CONNECTION

Your first attempt to access the Internet is always a tricky operation because you are required to set up a string of parameters. However, the data to be entered is too technical for most users. Another thing is that what works on your neighbour's machine does not necessarily work on yours. However, your Internet access provider should supply you with all the necessary information. Most go further and provide you with installation programs that handle the bulk of the work for you. Once you have set the Internet parameters, you do not have to reset them.

There are several ways to set up the log-on parameters:

- use the automated installation script supplied by your access provider;

- register a dial-up connection;

- use the Windows 98 Connection Wizard.

To a certain extent, the first method automates your dial-up networking. The second can be difficult but worth knowing. The third is more user-friendly. We shall now look at the last two options in detail.

SETTING UP A DIAL-UP CONNECTION

From My Computer, open the Dial-up Networking window and click Make New Connection. Make sure that you have first noted down all the relevant information you need to supply to your Internet access provider (you will need at least the telephone number of the Internet server you wish to call).

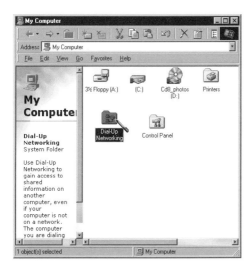

Figure 8.1: The Dial-up networking folder

As you will see, you can register several connections. Working in the Outlook Express messaging software, you can handle a number of mail and discussion forum accounts, if you so choose. Open the Dial-up Networking folder and click the Make New Connection icon. Then enter a name for your connection and give details of your modem. Now alter the settings by clicking Configure, if necessary. Enter the telephone number of the server for your access provider and confirm the information entered.

Figure 8.2: Entering the server telephone number for your access provider

The connection is marked by a new icon in the Dial-up Networking folder. Right-click this icon and select Properties. Next, click Server Types. Here you can change or define the Dial-up Server type (usually PPP for Windows) and check the communication protocols to be used. For the Internet, you must select TCP/IP.

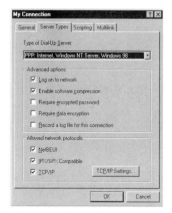

Figure 8.3: The type of Dial-up Server called

Next, click TCP/IP Settings to enter (where applicable) the server IP (Internet Protocol) addresses and the Internet address of the server. These addresses, in the form xxx.xxx.xxx.xxx (where x is a digit between 0 and 9), are forwarded by the access provider.

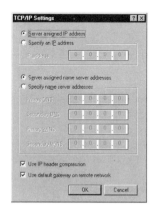

Figure 8.4: TCP/IP settings

At this stage, an Internet type connection can be set up with the server. But you should still configure the Internet Explorer browser and the Outlook Express messaging software to conduct interactive communications with the server resources (access to the Web, mail server access, etc.).

If the connection you have does not work, check your PC network settings based on the following.

The basic protocol

From the Control Panel, click the Network icon. Start the module to check that you have the following two lines at least:

- Dial-up access board;
- TCP/IP.

The first option simulates a Dial-up networking board, while TCP/IP is the general-purpose Internet exchange protocol.

TCP/IP settings

The software components and the Internet connection protocol are properly installed. Now you just need to check the server settings before you can access the Internet. To do this, select the TCP/IP line on the Network dialog box and click Properties.

The values you need to check (or enter) are under the Primary DNS (*Domain Name Server*) tab. These values are supplied by your Internet access provider. You should check the Primary DNS box and enter your address (or log-in) in the Host field, then enter the server name in the Domain box. Enter the identification of the name server in the DNS box. You should receive this information from your access provider. The name server translates an address of the type **aol.com** or **compuserve.com** into a physical address on the Internet network of the type "xxx.xxx.xxx.xxx". The name server also has a physical address that you should communicate to the log-on software.

This setting-up procedure is not easy: this is why it is preferable to fall back on the access provider installation procedure or, even better, to call up the Connection Wizard provided with Windows 98.

Check your Internet access provider options
Generally, the access provider procedure is designed for a specific browser. Get all the necessary details beforehand and make it clear that you will be using Windows 98 and Internet Explorer 4.0. If the set-up procedure was designed for Netscape, it will not work.

THE CONNECTION WIZARD

The Connection Wizard can be run from the Start menu. Click Programs, then the Internet Explorer folder and select Connection Wizard.

The Connection Wizard offers three types of installation:

- Opening a new Internet account. During this procedure, you will have to choose an access provider.

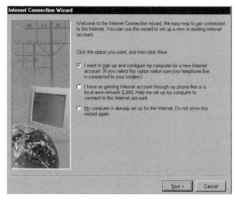

Figure 8.5: Running the Connection Wizard

- Adding a new connection via the telephone line or a local area network. You may have chosen an access provider, but you still have to tell the provider about the connection.

- Recognizing an Internet connection already on the computer.

Choose a provider and open an account

If you are not sure which access provider to choose, go for the first option mentioned above. Follow the procedure step-by-step. Set up your modem if you have not done so already. Tell the software where you are. It will then display a list of telephone numbers indicating the servers you can call. Choose a server near to you, so that you will be charged local telephone call charges.

The Connection Wizard will log on to the Microsoft Internet reference server and download a list of access providers near to you. The choice is yours.

Add a log-on account

Whether this is your first account or a new one, use the second option if you have already selected an Internet access provider. Then follow the procedure step-by-step.

First of all, state the nature of your connection:

- direct by modem, using a telephone line; or

- through a local area network.

Then select your modem. Enter the telephone number of your Internet access provider server. Next, enter your Internet user name and your password. Check beforehand with your provider whether you need to enter advanced settings: click Yes or No, as applicable.

Enter a name for your connection. This name will appear in the Dial-up Networking folder. The procedure then asks you if you want to configure your messaging account. Answer Yes and confirm by pressing the Next button. After that, enter your full name to send mail. Then, enter your future e-mail address (**name@server.domain**), which is the name allocated by your access provider.

Enter the mail server names (incoming and outgoing); usually, these are the same as the **mail.server.domain** names supplied by your provider.

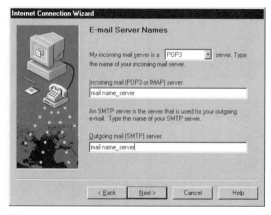

Figure 8.6: Entering the mail server name

Enter once again the name and password to log on to the server (these should be the same as you use to log on to the access provider). Then enter a name for your mail account, which will be used by the Outlook Express software.

By doing this you also usually install the news server (discussion groups) offered by your provider (of the **news.server.domain** type). Next, state whether you wish to have an entry in an Internet directory (or your corporate intranet).

You are now ready to log on to the Internet with your Web browser or your communications software: Outlook Express (for mail and forums) or NetMeeting or Microsoft Chat. Happy surfing!

Before we discuss the Internet browser in depth (in Hour 9), you will also be able to use the Web channels available through Windows 98, those situated on your active Desktop.

WEB CHANNELS

The channel concept, developed by Microsoft in Windows 98, is an application that uses Push Technology, as opposed to Pull. This is where you head for information by using your favourite search engine, or else the information will come to you (with your permission, of course) without any effort on your part, except that you will need to choose paths or information channels and schedule the arrival of the information on your PC.

With Web channels, also known as *Active Channels*, Microsoft has introduced a new way of using the Web. The basic concept helps you call up information by arranging it in a more logical way on your Desktop.

Subscriptions and downloading sites are similar concepts in Windows 98. The difference between a Web channel and any other Web site you can subscribe to are of a purely technical and marketing nature. The Web channels comply with a standard developed by Microsoft, known as *Channel Definition Format* (CDF). They rely on a shared subscription button; some have preferential agreements with Microsoft which allow them to appear on the Desktop from the moment you install Windows 98.

The major novelty of Web channels lies in the combination of the medium and the message, the carrier and the contents, the software tool and the Web sites. For the first time, the user is offered not only software tools and functions, but also multimedia content: in total, eleven active channels are projected onto your Desktop, including BBC Online, Financial Times and Vogue.

Figure 8.7: The "remote control" or channel bar previewed on the Windows Desktop

There is also the Microsoft Channel Guide, a facility that steers you through all the channels available on the Web. The scope of channel viewing is not confined to the initial start-up facilities, which favour UK content, but extends to Web channels worldwide.

HOW TO SUBSCRIBE

It is easy to subscribe to a channel displayed on the Desktop. First of all, click one of the eleven buttons on offer. In our example, we have chosen New Scientist.

A single click on New Scientist on the channel bar connects you to the Internet: the welcome page opens in the Internet Explorer browser. This reveals a blue button: Add Active Channel. Click on this to start the process. As we have seen, Add to Active Desktop enables you to position the New Scientist service in any other location on your Windows 98 Desktop.

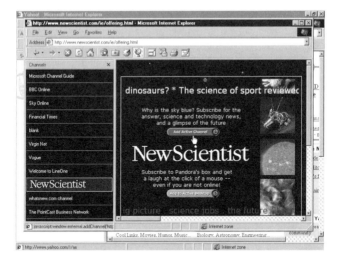

Figure 8.8: The welcome page for the New Scientist channel

Now you just need to click Add Active Channel to run the subscription sequence for the chosen channel. The update procedure begins and then the subscription management window opens.

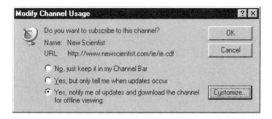

Figure 8.9: The channel subscription procedure

You are offered three choices:

- No immediate subscription, but you still have channel bar access

- You would like to be notified of channel updates

- You would like to be notified, but you can decide to download the channel content to examine it off-line.

If you choose the third option, you can program the downloading frequency and times. You could also fall back on the scheduling proposed by the channel publisher. From this point on all the scheduling data will be collected by the Subscription Wizard. Click Customize to alter the channel settings, then press OK to start the subscription process.

LOOKING FOR NEW CHANNELS

There are two ways of looking for channels that are not displayed on the Windows 98 Desktop. Either you find a channel when surfing the Web using the Add Active Channel button. You then click to start the subscription procedure; or you can use the on-line guide, or *Active Channel Guide,* to search for a channel.

The on-line guide

Click on Channel Guide on the channel bar. You can search by entering a subject from the five offered (information and technology, business, sport, entertainment, lifestyles and travel).

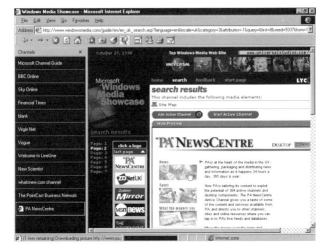

Figure 8.10: The results of a search using the channel guide

At this point, you can search channels throughout the world. To do so, click Options.

Under each of the options proposed, you can carry out a universal search of:

- All languages;
- All countries; or
- All subjects.

One you have selected the options, click Search. The channel icons are shown on the left; point at a logo to view a brief description of the channel.

When you right-click and select Subscription, you can either:

- take out a subscription; or
- add the channel to your Favorites.

Hour 9

The Internet Explorer browser

THE CONTENTS FOR THIS HOUR

- Internet Explorer 4.0
- Running the browser
- Working on-line or off-line
- The main principles of browsing
- Searching the Web
- Managing your favourite Web sites
- Programmed downloading of Web pages and sites

Internet Explorer 4.0, a software package distributed free by Microsoft, is already installed with the Windows 98 operating system. With this new version, the software leads the way to new Internet standards: Dynamic HTML, XML, CDF (*Channel Definition Format*), OSD (*Open Software Description*), ECMA Script, or even Java.

Included among the significant advances offered by Internet Explorer, we might note the following:

- It is a far more powerful browser than its predecessor, Internet Explorer 3.0.

- It has a better approach to Internet security (security areas, certificates, Authenticode technology, etc.).

- It uses Dynamic HTML (as well as HTML 3.2 and HTML 4.0).

- It has better integration of the Java language.

- It uses "push" technology support by way of channels.

- It incorporates advanced communication tools for personal or business needs (audio and videoconferencing; groupware) with, amongst others, NetMeeting.

- It has increased recognition of messaging standards (SMPT/POP3, NNTP, IMAP4, LDAP, MIME, S/MIME) in Outlook Express.

- It has centralized management of several messaging, mail and news accounts.

- It manages continuous multimedia traffic streams (audio and video) with NetShow and RealPlayer from Progressive Networks.

- It supports traditional audio formats (AIFF, AU, MIDI and WAV) and video formats (AVI, QuickTime), but also MPEG format (audio/video), VRML (interactive 3D) and ASF (NetShow).

To these features, we should add the Web development tools:

- Front Page Express (for designing Web pages); and

- Personal Web Server (for publishing a personal site).

Once your Internet connection has been set up you can surf the Web using all the resources your browser offers.

RUNNING THE BROWSER

The Web navigation program, Internet Explorer 4.0, can be called up from the Start menu (Programs, Internet Explorer folder). You can also use the shortcut displayed on the Desktop or you can use the Quick Launch bar (to the right of the Start button) on the Taskbar.

When the browser opens, the default home page is displayed (this is a page from a Microsoft site) as soon as you have accepted the invitation to start the Internet log-on procedure (see Hour 5 for log-on settings).

Your home page

By default, the browser is configured to display a Microsoft site, but you can display any site you choose as your home page by clicking Display and then Internet Options. In the General dialog box, enter the URL (address) of your home page and confirm your choice by clicking Default Page. When you next run the browser, this is the page that will be displayed by default. In particular, you can quote a reference for your favourite search engine. In a company, you can also quote a reference for its intranet welcome page, which gives access to all its internal communication services.

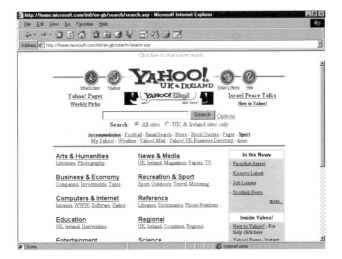

Figure 9.1: Opening the browser with a display of the default page; in this case, the Yahoo search engine

You might decide to work off-line and display Web pages stored locally or recorded using the History facility. If you find that a particular page is not available, a dialog box will invite you to log on.

If you decide to remain off-line, the Work Off-line facility is active in the browser File menu. You may at any time deselect this option or activate the Connection button in the dialog boxes.

In on-line mode, the connection to a page which is not available is set up automatically when you call up a page.

Figure 9.2: Starting up an Internet connection

If you click Cancel, the connection attempt is interrupted and the browser opens the dial-up networking window. You can alter the log-on settings (Settings button), if you wish, or choose to stay off-line, or resume the connection procedure. If several users share the PC, it is at this point that you enter your log-on password.

Figure 9.3: Entering your password (optional)

The password can be registered by checking the Password Registration box; from this point on, you will not need to enter it again.

Windows 98

Are you ready to connect to the Internet?
If your Internet log on settings have not yet been configured, you can call up Internet Options from the Display menu. Click the Log-on tab and then select Connection. This brings up the Connection Wizard. You can use it as a reference for your first Internet account (to call up an access provider) or a new access account or to gain access via a local area network. For further details, refer to Hour 8.

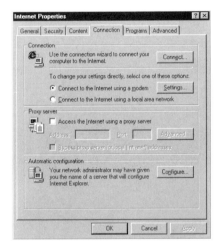

Figure 9.4: Internet log-on options; click Connection to run the Wizard

Establishing or terminating your Internet connection

Most of the time, the log-on start-up routine is automated. Entering a Web address in the entry box or asking for a page update is sufficient for the browser to invite you to accept the connection.

Establishing your connection before running the browser
*You can establish your Internet connection routine before you
run the browser. Just open My Computer, then select Dial-up
Networking. Next, start the log-on sequence by clicking the
icon representing your Internet access provider, or any one
of your providers if you have several accounts. Then click
Connection in the Connect To window. You can also select the
Connection icon (without clicking) and press Dial.*

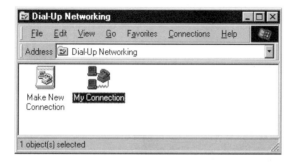

*Figure 9.5: The Dial-up Networking folder and the
specified connections*

*Figure 9.6: Starting the Internet connection routine
without the browser*

Once you have established your connection, you can run your browser and surf the Web. A connection indicator is visible on the Taskbar (to the right).

To log off, right-click on the active connection icon and select Log off.

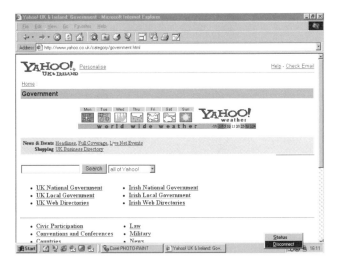

Figure 9.7: The connection has been established; click Status to display the log-on status or Disconnect

When you click Status, you can check the speed of the log-on process and the quantity of data interchanged between the server and your PC, as well as the time elapsed.

BROWSING PRINCIPLES

Since everything begins with an address, enter one in the address bar (just under the toolbar). The address of your company, for instance, might be **http://www.enterprise.com**. If you enter the address incorrectly, either because it no longer exists or because you mistyped it, you will be alerted. The error message 'nffl 404' means that the URL is not known.

The navigation buttons

If the address proves to be correct, the page requested is displayed. You can then browse from that first page by clicking on the active links offered. The browser stores the pages displayed previously. To go back to the previous page, click Back on the toolbar. After you have gone back, you can display the following pages again by clicking Forward.

When loading a page, the browser icon (which is shown in reduced size at the top right of your browser screen) moves; at the same time, the information and the objects being loaded are shown on the status bar (at the bottom of the browser). When the page has been loaded, the icon stops moving.

You progress from one page to the next, from one site to another, or one service to another (and, sometimes, even from one country to another) by clicking on the links offered. These links can assume all sorts of different shapes on a Web page. They are active areas and your browser shows them clearly by changing the appearance of the mouse cursor; the arrow becomes a hand, meaning that you can access another page.

You may often wish to return to a particular page. You can click several times on Back to return, or ask for the last list to be displayed by clicking on the small down arrow to the right of the Back button. A list of pages is displayed with their names. This is a practical way of quickly accessing a specific page.

See Fig 9.8 p44
PTO

Figure 9.8: A list of pages displayed previously

The History file

Another method, which is equally practical, consists of displaying the History file. This has a much wider range since it stores details of your browsing over several log on sessions. To display the History file, click on History on the toolbar. The History pane opens to the left of the browser. You can pick a specific date or display all the visits you have made earlier in the day.

If you click on a particular site, the pages of that site are then also listed. If you change sites, the previous list is closed and the list of pages at the new site is shown.

Displaying links

When a list is offered in the conventional way (underlined text), you can check whether it has been used previously. This allows you, on a page with a number of links, to determine which links you might want to explore. The link colour changes the moment you use it. The colours of links that have and have not been activated can be programmed. Just go to the Internet Options feature in the Display menu, click on the General dialog box and then select Colors at the bottom of the box.

Here, you can define the colours for:

- Links not used;

- Links used;

- Highlighting a link when the mouse pointer passes over it: simply check the Select by pointing box.

By clicking on a colour box, you bring up a display of the palette: select the colour you want.

▬▬▬ Full-screen surfing

Internet Explorer 4.0 allows you to browse in full-screen mode. Apart from a small icon bar at the top of the screen, the entire visible surface of your monitor can be used to display Web pages. In this way, you can make the most of the sites you have visited.

To switch to full-screen mode, click Full screen on the toolbar. The vertical and horizontal risers only appear if the Web page is longer or wider than your display. Not only has the browser environment been reduced, the Taskbar (at the bottom of the screen) has also disappeared from the screen at the same time.

To return to classic style, click on the same minimized icon on the reduced-size toolbar in full screen mode.

Total full screen
To obtain a total full screen, you need to hide the reduced-size full screen bar. To do this, click a free area on the toolbar and select Hide Automatically. The bar then disappears: it will not be displayed again until you point the mouse cursor to the top of the screen.

In the total full-screen mode, you can go back to the previous page or display the next by opening the context-sensitive menu: right-click on a non-active area of the current Web page.

Opening Web pages in a new window

It is possible to alter the way in which the results of all your Web requests are opened in the browser window, and to switch from one page to the next by pressing the Forward and Back buttons. This enables you to open pages in a new browser window. From the File menu, select New and then Window: a new browser window opens. You can then switch between browsing operations in several windows without mixing up the Web pages you have received.

Another option consists of opening a link, chosen from a Web page, in a new window. To do this, right-click on the link in question: a context-sensitive menu is displayed, in which you select Open in New Window.

Figure 9.9: Opening a link in a new window

All sorts of links
Usually, a link is shown as underlined text. But Web programming also allows a link to be assigned to an action button, a graphic or a map. A graphic can even comprise several links, depending on the place in which you click the mouse button. A drop-down list might also offer a series of access links. On certain Web pages, you can find specific icons representing the next or previous pages, inviting the user to browse a series of screens.

The explorer bar

The explorer bar opens to the left of the browser and allows you to view Web pages on the right-hand side of the screen, whilst you carry out searches and select options in the right-hand list. Of the lists offered, you will find History, Favorites, Channels and search results. You can access all these lists by clicking on the relevant button on the toolbar.

You can close the explorer bar by clicking on the cross at the top right of the frame. If the list is long, you can use the down arrow to display the rest of the links on offer and the up arrow to go back up the list.

A list contains objects; in other words, folders or addresses. When you click on a folder, you open a sub-menu which is a list of the addresses entered in the folder. In your Favorites, a document is a subject (Hobbies, Finance, etc.) that you have defined in order to classify your Web sites to suit your particular tastes. In History, there are three organisational levels: the enquiry day (or week), the site visited and the pages you looked up at a given site.

WEB SURFING

To start a search, click on Search. The explorer bar opens and, if you are off-line, the Internet connection procedure begins. The operating mode is the same as that described for the new features of Windows 98 Explorer. The search module displays a page at the Microsoft site with a group of search engines.

Using the Favorites search tools
You can continue searching using the tools selected on the Web. Beforehand, you should have specified the search engines that you find the most interesting in a Favorites folder. If you have done this, click on Favorites, select the relevant folder and click on one of the search engines. In this case the search results will not be displayed in the explorer bar, but on the overall page sent back by the search engine server.

The Back and Forward buttons do not operate in the Explorer pane, but only in the main part of the browser. To conduct a new search with the same search engine, type the new keyword(s) in the search area and click Search. To conduct a search with another search engine, click on Click here at the top of the Explorer pane to begin a fresh search. This is not always a particularly practical method and you might prefer to use the Web search engines in the conventional way. Some of them even suggest on their results page a different search engine you can use to conduct your search.

MANAGING YOUR FAVOURITE WEB SITES

The first of your favourite sites is your home site. You have seen how it is possible to enter Web areas on the Desktop in the same way as the channels offered as standard in Windows 98, and you can even choose an HTML page as a background which would point to one of your favourite sites. But the most common method of keeping a record of the pages you have visited is to store them in your Favorites folder. Favorites are folders and lists of links that you can easily open and activate at any time.

Storing your Favorites

To record a Web site in your Favorites, select the Favorites menu and click Add to Favorites. You are now presented with a number of options:

- storing the page directly (or the link to the page) in the Favorites root directory;

- storing it in an existing folder (a page on the cinema, for instance, would be stored in a Cinema folder, another on holidays would be stored in Travel folder, etc.);

- creating a new folder for a new Web page subject.

Figure 9.10: Adding a Favorite

You can give a new name to the Web page you want to record in your Favorites. If the title is not self-explanatory, or if it is in another language, you can change its title. Click OK and the page will be stored in the root directory. In the list of Favorites it will be visible at the end of the list after any folders. A good method is to store the pages systematically in folders and to define in advance (or when needed) the folder types.

To store a page in a folder, click Create in the store window. Two options are presented:

- The folder exists. Locate it in the list (but be careful, the list is a tree structure; a folder may contain other folders) and select it; then click OK to confirm.

- The folder does not exist. Go to the place where you want to create it (in the Favorites root directory or another folder); click New, enter the filename and confirm.

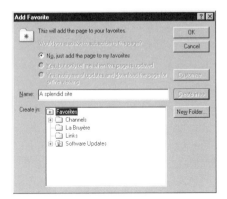

Figure 9.11: Storing a Web page in a Favorites folder

You can go even further when arranging your Favorites and, when storing a page, ask to be notified of any changes made to the page. If you want to do this, click the second option. The third option relates to a programmed subscription to a site (for downloading and off-line reading).

Re-arranging your Favorites

As time goes by, you might need to tidy your Favorites or re-arrange them. You can delete a favourite site, a complete folder or even transfer a particular folder to another. To do this, select the Favorites menu and click Organize Favorites. Then click a folder: you can now delete it, rename it, open it to fetch specific links or move it to another location.

Scheduled downloading from a Web site

You can decide to subscribe to a site: simply check 'Yes, notify me of updates and download the page for offline viewing' box. Then click Customize to set your subscription parameters. The Subscriptions Wizard will then do the rest.

Figure 9.12: The Wizard for subscribing to a Web page or site

You can opt to download a Web page or part of the site (the page itself and any linked pages). To do this, check one of the two options offered. Click Forward to confirm. You can decide to receive an e-mail message advising you of a change to the page (or one of the pages). Click No if you do not want this option.

Figure 9.13: Option to be notified by e-mail of any Web page changes

You can now adapt the download settings by indicating the downloading frequency (every day, every week, etc.). You can even devise a personal schedule:

- by setting the downloading frequency (daily, weekly, monthly); and

- by stating the download time (Modify button).

The Subscriptions Wizard asks you to define a schedule. Check this box and click New to create a new schedule. You can devise as many schedules as you wish and assign them on the basis of the sites to be downloaded. To change the settings of a particular schedule, click Modify.

Avoid bottlenecks
There is always the possibility that a number of Web surfers have made the same programming choices as you have at the same sites. If you have problems logging on at a certain time, accept a programming variation. To do this, check the 'Vary the exact time of the next update' box for better results in the Personalized Scheduling window.

Once your schedule settings have been entered and accepted, the Wizard asks if you want to set a password. This is useful in an office environment if you would prefer, when you are away, that no-one else can pick up confidential information downloaded to your PC. Answer No if no access control is required and click Close. Finally, you need to confirm the addition of this site to your Favorites.

You can then handle all your subscriptions via the Subscriptions window. To access it, select the Favorites menu and click Manage Subscriptions.

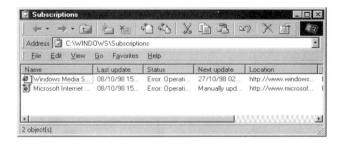

Figure 9.14: Handling all subscriptions to Web sites

From the Subscriptions window, you can check, amend or cancel subscriptions. Right-click on one of the service links and select Properties. The subscription Properties window allows you to adjust:

- the reception settings; and
- the scheduling settings.

Hour 10

Electronic mail

THE CONTENTS FOR THIS HOUR

- Handling your mail (sending and receiving)
- Personalising your messages
- Handling the Address Book
- Sending and receiving secure messages
- Reading your mail from more than one computer

Windows 98 is supplied and installed complete with an electronic mail software package known as Outlook Express. Electronic mail, or e-mail, as it is more widely known, is the most frequently used Internet tool. Apart from looking up Web sites, the ability to forward messages and handle mail efficiently is one of the chief concerns of users.

Whether you use this facility in a private or business capacity, e-mail has become an indispensable tool.

Users of Internet Explorer 4.0 (in Windows 95) may already have tried out Outlook Express. The software operates as a communications centre, managing, sending and receiving e-mail and messages from discussion groups. It incorporates an Address Book and offers a wide range of features. Outlook Express replaces the communications centre offered in Windows 95,which was known as Microsoft Exchange. It is a program for sending messages and joining discussion groups, using Internet standards. It represents a merger between Internet Mail and Internet News, which is a considerable step forward. Outlook Express allows you to configure your connection settings and manage mail with great efficiency, also enabling you to handle several Internet accounts. This is of value when you link a business account and a personal account; it is also practical in terms of sharing software at home.

As with any browser, the mail software can be called up from the Start menu, on the Desktop, or from the Quick Launch bar on the Taskbar.

The main software screen shows the following components:

- the toolbar;
- the mail document folders in the left-hand column (the display pane);
- access to major software features in the main frame.

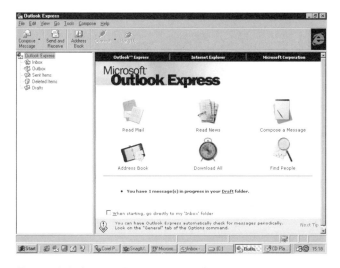

Figure 10.1: Outlook Express mail software

When using the software for the first time, five default folders are available:

- **the Inbox.** This should not be confused with the icon bearing the same name in the Windows 95 Exchange software.

- **the Outbox.** This contains all the mail written off-line or to be sent later.

- **the Sent Items folder.** This keeps a record of messages sent.

- **the Deleted Items folder.** When a file is deleted it is sent temporarily to this folder, unless you have configured the software settings differently. Remember to regularly clear out messages in this folder or request that the data be deleted when you quit the software.

- **the Drafts folder.** This is a holding folder in which mail you are currently working on can be kept temporarily.

There may be an additional folder for the discussion forums proposed by the Internet access provider.

HANDLING YOUR MESSAGES EFFECTIVELY

The Inbox may be less practical when you are dealing with a large number of messages. If you communicate with a large number of people, if your e-mail is published on Web sites or other media, or if you subscribe to information services supplied by e-mail, you will soon find out just how restrictive your single mailbox is. You therefore need to create new folders to store messages received (or, at least, those you wish to keep).

▬▬▬ Creating document folders

Outlook Express enables you handle a folder tree structure easily and to despatch your messages by subject. In this way, you can create an initial personal folder and another for business if you have a multi-purpose account.

To create a new document folder, right-click on the Outlook Express root directory on the software explorer bar. Select OPEN in the context-sensitive menu and activate the New folder command. Give the folder a name and then place it amongst the tree structure of existing folders.

By doing this, you can create a new folder in an existing folder.

Figure 10.2: Creating a document folder

▆▆▆ Handling the arrival of new messages

By this stage, your Internet connection settings have been configured and your access provider server should be correctly identified. When starting up Outlook Express, the connection may be set up automatically, or you can log-on at your request. You can also specify a start-up without logging on. This allows you, for example, to prepare mail off-line, place it in the Outbox and initiate a bulk despatch once you are on-line. In this way, you save on the cost of your calls. But you might also decide to start up the Internet connection every time you open the program in order to retrieve any new messages. To do this, go to the Tools menu and click Options. Select the Dial-up connection tab and check the chosen option.

You can configure other settings from the General tab in the Options window. For instance, you can also check the arrival of new messages every hour. This is the dialog box in which you define your default mail reading routine. You can ask to be notified at regular intervals by checking the first option proposed. Irrespective of the automatic procedures you may have instituted to read your mail, you can also open your e-mail box at any time by clicking on Send and Receive on the Outlook Express toolbar.

When you click Send and Receive, the Send function is initiated first. All the messages that may be stored in the Outbox are then sent, so make sure you have drafted them properly (the right spelling, attachments present, etc.). If some messages are incomplete, ideally you should store them in the Drafts folder before moving them to the Outbox.

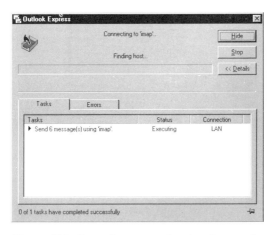

Figure 10.3: Once the connection has been set up, this working window shows message transfers in progress (messages sent and received)

The Details button in the above figure provides information on the tasks performed and any problems arising. If, on completion, the Hang Up button is checked, your line is disconnected automatically when the sending tasks have been finished and you have received any messages waiting.

Check your connection
From the Tools menu, check Accounts and, in the Internet Accounts window, select the Mail tab. Your access provider's (also known as an Internet Service Provider, or ISP) mail server references are shown here. The Properties button enables you to fine-tune your settings, if necessary.

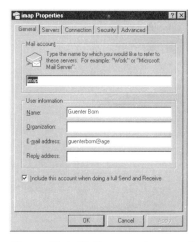

Figure 10.4: Mail account properties

Looking up your messages

To look up messages received, point the mouse to the Inbox. This setting is either automatic when the application starts up, or you need to click the Inbox in the left-hand pane to access it. A list of the message headers received is shown in the right-hand frame and, at the bottom of the window, you will see the contents of the message selected in the list.

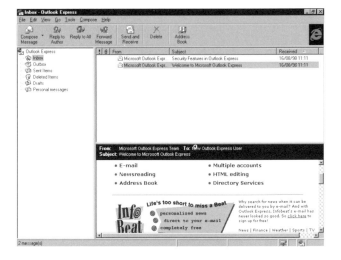

Figure 10.5: Looking up messages received

The Inbox structure is based on five components:

- the degree of urgency of the message (an exclamation mark (!) in red, means an important message is waiting);

- attached items (if the "paperclip" icon is showing in this column);

- the name of the sender;

- the subject of the message;

- the date and time of receipt.

Messages highlighted in bold have not yet been read. The number of unread messages is also indicated, in brackets, in the Inbox. The contents of the selected message are displayed in the bottom portion of the screen.

Display an attached document
The software tells you if a document has been attached, by displaying the paperclip icon. Click on the message in question and then, in the reading area, click the paperclip. The list of attachments is displayed. Click one of them and, depending on the document format, the appropriate software will be run. A .doc file will be displayed in Word and a .ppt file in PowerPoint, etc.

Transferring a message

You can transfer a message from the Inbox to a storage file using the drag-and-drop facility. Similarly, you can right-click on the message and ask to move it. The same menu also allows you to transfer the message in question to someone else. To transfer a message you have received to another person, click Transfer Message on the toolbar. A send window opens, and you then specify the addressee.

Deleting a message

To delete a message, activate the Delete command in the context-sensitive menu, or click Delete on the toolbar. Items deleted are actually copied to the Deleted Items folder. This is emptied when you quit the Outlook Express program, provided you specified this when configuring the Options settings (General dialog box).
In the same place, you should check the Empty Deleted Items folder box as you exit. If you do not check this box, the messages are never actually deleted. From time to time you should clear out the Deleted Items folder to stop your hard disk getting clogged up unnecessarily. When you right-click on the Deleted Items folder, you can activate the Empty Folder command.

Sorting messages

You may find it useful to sort the messages in your Inbox or any document folder. By default, messages are stacked in date order: the one with the most recent date is at the top of the stack, or at the head of the list. To sort the messages, click the bar in the (From/ Subject/Received) field. When you click Sender (From), you sort the messages by name in ascending order. When you click a second time, you reverse the order of the sort to descending order. You can revert to the initial sort by clicking Received.

You can also sort messages and put them into 'urgent' groupings, or group those with an attachment (these are the first two fields on the field bar above the list). The sort functions can be called up from the View menu, by activating the Sort By command.

Drafting a message

To compose a message, click Draft Message on the Outlook Express toolbar. Complete the Addressee, Copy to, and Message subject fields, then type the message.

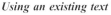

Using an existing text
You can prepare a message using the Windows Notepad, Drafts, or your usual word processor. Select the text, copy it (Ctrl-C) and, when you get back to the message drafting window, paste it in (Ctrl-V).

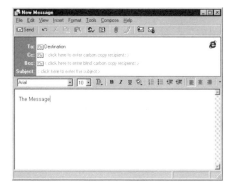

Figure 10.6: The message drafting window

To enter the addressee's details, you can type just the first few letters of his name. If there is a reference to him in the Address Book, the Input Wizard suggests a complete name; click the icon to the left of the input line to open the Address Book. Select your addressee. In the same way, you can specify those whom you wish to receive a copy (Cc: carbon copy). Their names can be seen by the other addressees. To hide the recipients of copies, use the line Bcc (blind carbon copy).

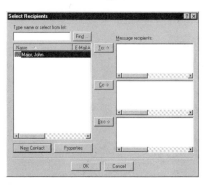

Figure 10.7: Choosing a message recipient in the Address Book

Inserting a link in a mail message

*To insert a link, select the text to be converted to a link. This may be the link expression in uncoded form or a key expression, such as **http://www.company.uk** or even "the company", then click on the Link to Insert icon. In the input window, enter the name of the link. This will be displayed with the usual hypertext link attributes (colours, underlining, etc.). Your call partner can click on the link to display the Web page or contact another person by e-mail. In the latter case, use the Mail To command, followed by the address of the person to contact.*

Inserting a picture in a mail message

To insert a picture, click the icon at the far right of the message drafting toolbar. In the working window that then opens, enter the path to the picture file or browse the hard disk to locate it, then confirm. The picture appears in the message drafting window. You can select it, move it and resize it as you wish.

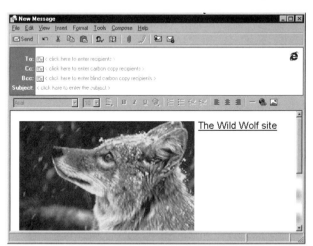

Figure 10.8: A message containing a picture and a hypertext link

The right format

If the person you are e-mailing cannot handle HTML format, your message may be appended as an attachment, or the enhancements may be lost. Check out the details beforehand. To get the most out of the enhancements, make sure the settings are configured correctly. Ensure that the Reply to Messages using their Original Format option has been checked on the Send tab in the Options window of the Tools menu.

Once you have composed your message, click Send or, from the File menu, the Send later option. A message waiting to be sent starts the dialling sequence to the Internet access provider if you are not logged on. A message to be sent later is kept on hold in the Outbox. It will be sent, along with any others, the next time you activate Send or Receive on the software toolbar.

Inserting an attachment

One of the best insertion features is the ability to insert an attached document. You can append as many files as you wish to your outgoing mail; you can send a text written in Word, a photograph, or an Excel spreadsheet.

To insert a file, select the Insert menu. Click on Attachment and browse the hard disk to find the file you want. Repeat the operation as many times as you need.

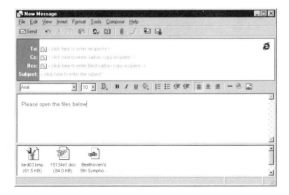

Figure 10.9 : Attached documents are displayed at the bottom of the message drafting window. In this case, three files (text, a picture and music) are appended, with details of their respective sizes

The sizes of the attached files are summarized at the bottom of the message drafting window. This is useful to know, because a file that is too bulky can take quite a time to be despatched and especially to receive. Do not overload the message if there is no need to do so. You will save your addressee a very long recieving time.

THE ADDRESS BOOK

It is time-consuming when you have to enter the electronic address of a person you wish to contact. This task can be carried out by the Outlook Express Address Book. This feature of the software supplies you with the Internet addresses of your contacts. We have come across the Address Book earlier; let us go back to how it works.

Handling the Address Book

Click on Address Book in the Outlook Express toolbar to open it. You can also do this from the Internet Explorer browser by selecting the Go to menu, followed by Address Book. Another way of

opening it is via the message drafting window; to do so, click on
the icon opposite:

- Recipient;

- Copy;

- Hidden copy.

The Address Book contains the electronic addresses of your
contacts, together with their telephone numbers or street addresses.

Figure 10.10: The Address Book

Adding a new contact

You can add a contact manually by clicking New Contact on the
toolbar. You should enter the name and electronic address in the
Personal dialog box, but you could also enter details of the home
or office or contact information via NetMeeting software. You can
also give a certificate referecnce for the contact in question.

Figure 10.11 : Entering details of a new contact

Filling in the Address Book automatically

There are two ways of adding a contact to your Address Book:

- manually, when you receive a message from a new contact; or

- part-automatically for each new contact you reply to.

This is what you do in the first case:

1. Position the mouse cursor on the message in question.

2. Right-click on the Open command to activate it, or double-click.

3. Point the mouse to the name of the sender.

4. Click the right button to display the context-sensitive menu.

5. Select Add to Address Book.

6. The Add contact window opens with the default Forename, Surname and E-mail fields.

7. Make the necessary adjustments and confirm.

Adding a contact automatically
You can also automate the add new contacts function as
follows: select the Tools menu, choose Options, then click
if necessary on the General tab and check the 'Automatically
add the people I reply to in my Address Book' box and
confirm the entire sequence.

Setting up an electronic mailshot

You can group your contacts under a single entry. This enables
you to send the same message to a group of people. In this way,
you can define work groups or communities with a common activity.
It is a good way of working in groups or sending mailshots by
E-mail.

FILTERING MESSAGES

You can process messages received and, depending on their contents
and source, you can automate particular tasks. To do this, start
from the Tools menu and click Inbox Assistant.

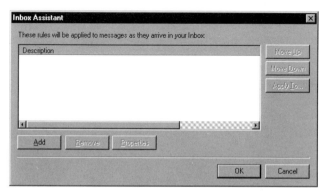

Figure 10.12: Calling up the Inbox Assistant

From the Assistant window, click Add in order to create a new mail management rule. At this point, you can define conditions relating to the incoming message:

- the destination (To);
- the people who are to receive copies;
- the source (From);
- the subject.

If one or more of these areas contains the information specified, you can initiate certain actions automatically, such as:

- transferring the message to a document folder;
- copying the message to a folder;
- transferring the message to another contact;
- preventing the message from being downloaded from the server;
- overriding the server.

Handling your subscriptions effectively
If you subscribe to an on-line information service, you might find it useful to file the messages automatically in the same document folder. Use the Systematic option for the subject or sender as a condition and ask for the message to be moved to the folder. In this way, your Inbox will not be filled by subscriptions that you can read at your leisure from your customised folder.

READING YOUR MAIL FROM MORE THAN ONE COMPUTER

To manage your mail correctly from a portable or desktop PC, you must retain it on the server when you look it up from the portable and copy it to the desktop PC for centralized reception. Actually,

by default, the messages are copied from the server to the PC it is connected to. With these settings, the mail will be distributed amongst the various machines, depending on the connections set up. You cannot possibly get a central view of your messages under such conditions. To block deletion of the message at the server end on one of the PCs, this is how you need to configure your software:

1. Activate the Tools menu.

2. Select Accounts.

3. In the Internet Accounts window, click the Mail tab.

4. Select your mail server.

5. Click Properties.

6. Select the Advanced tab.

7. In the Delivery area, check the Leave a copy of messages on server box.

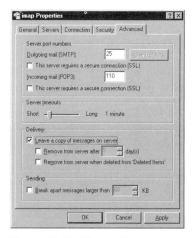

Figure 10.13: The mail remains stored in the server

You can also ask for mail to be deleted after a specified number of days or initiate deletion when the messages have been deleted from the Deleted Items folder in Outlook Express (two additional options in the Delivery area).

Hour 11

System tools

THE CONTENTS FOR THIS HOUR

- Scheduled tasks
- System information
- The system file troubleshooter
- Tidying up the hard disk
- The FAT 32 converter
- Defragmenting the disk
- Backing-up data
- Checking the disk with Scandisk
- DriveSpace 3 and the compression agent

Windows 98 is considered to be more powerful than its predecessor, Windows 95. With more high-performance settings and a faster shutdown, the day-to-day operation of Windows has been greatly improved. As we saw in the installation procedure, this operation includes technical monitoring of the PC to enhance performance and prevent problems.

SCHEDULED TASKS

Tasks scheduled at installation time can be altered later. To do this, open the Scheduled Tasks folder from My Computer. These tasks can also be called up from the Start menu, by selecting Programs, Accessories, then System tools.

Figure 11.1: The scheduled system tasks folder

Then check a task, point the mouse to the icon, then right-click and ask for Properties. Three dialog boxes are displayed:

- a task general description dialog box;

- the programming schedule;

- additional settings.

In Settings, for instance, you can ask for a task to be deleted as soon as it has finished running. You can also halt the task at the end of a specified time limit.

You can also set the following rules:

- task start-up can only begin if the machine has been idle for x minutes;

- if the PC is currently in use, you may decide not to run the task.

Finally, you can also optimize the power supply resources (in the case of portables) so that:

- the task will not start if the PC is running on a battery; or

- the task shuts down as soon as the PC switches to battery mode.

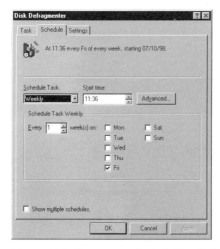

Figure 11.2: The task schedule for Disk Defragmenter

In this way, you can modify or delete existing tasks. The Create as Scheduled task icon enables you to run the Scheduled Task Wizard.

Figure 11.3: The Scheduled Task Wizard

Once the Wizard is up and running, click the programs you wish to run in Windows 98. References to all the programs resident in the PC exist in a window to which you simply point in order to run any of them automatically. Thus, you can select Outlook Express to schedule your mail reading routine. You indicate the frequency with which you want to run the program: every day, for example; you then set the start time.

Once you have configured the settings, check the 'Open Advance Properties for this Task when you click the Close' box. You are then able to limit the task execution time. On completion of the settings, the task is added to the Scheduled Tasks folder. Windows 98 now stays on continuous alert, ready to run the tasks you requested.

THE SYSTEM SOFTWARE

This can be accessed from the Start menu, through Programs, Accessories, then System tools. Here you will find a number of tools that were supplied with Windows 95. Some have been upgraded, whilst others are new.

The new tools are as follows:

- the FAT 32 drive converter
- the disk purge facility
- system information
- the system file checker
- windows Set-up (the program run at installation).

This last program allows you to modify settings and set-up times. When you click Set-up now, the software runs all the system tasks pre-programmed at installation (see Hour 2) or modified subsequently.

The following tools have been upgraded:

- the disk defragmenter; and
- the backup facility.

Tools such as Scandisk (checking the file allocation tables, the files themselves and the surface state of the hard disk) or DriveSpace (disk compression facility) remain unchanged. You can, however, schedule Scandisk to check the files and the disk drives in the PC.

Figure 11.4: Windows 98 system tools

System information

Windows 98 incorporates a System Information 4.1 utility, which provides an overview of resources, components and the software environment. This tool is more sophisticated than the system icon accessed from the Control Panel in Windows 95 (but this is still available in Windows 98).

The pane on the left allows you to access the information headings, whilst the pane on the right displays the system data.

This utility contains a series of ActiveX checks which collect the information requested and display it in the software.

This tool is very powerful and enables you to carry out quick technical checks. If there is an operating problem with the PC, it can be used to detect any fault or a pilot version problem.

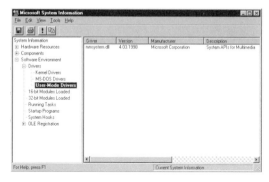

Figure 11.5: The software environment data; in this case, the User-mode Drivers

The system file Checker

This program checks that all the system files are correct. It also enables you to fetch a file from the Windows 98 installation CD-ROM in order to replace a defective system file.

Before running the checker, click Settings to configure the system as necessary. In this way, you can specify the file backup method before any restoration begins. Three options are available:

- routine backup before restoration;
- backup on demand (confirmation message);
- no backup.

The Settings dialog box also lets you keep a log. This file keeps a record of the checks and modifications you have made.

Click the Search Element tab to establish:

- the folders and sub-folders to be examined;
- the types of file (extension) to be examined.

Tidying up the hard disk

A further new utility is the disk cleaning tool. On start-up, this software determines the spaces it can purge and therefore release on the hard disk. The Disk Cleanup window opens and indicates the volume (in megabytes) that can be released for each type of file. The evaluations are divided into file types:

- temporary Internet files;
- files downloaded from the network;
- files sent to the Recycle Bin;
- femporary files; and
- Windows 98 uninstall information files.

Uninstalling Windows 98
Do not purge the Windows 98 uninstall files if you think you might want to revert to your old operating system at a later stage.

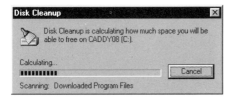

Figure 11.6: Determining disk space that can be released

The More options tab in the purging window is used either to delete unused Windows 98 installation files, or to erase programs that are no longer used (an old game, or an electronic office package that has become obsolete).

In the latter case, the software starts up the program uninstall window, with which we were familiar in Windows 95 and which is still available in the Windows 98 Control Panel.

182

The FAT 32 converter

This program is designed to convert the File Allocation Tables (FAT) to 32-bit format, thus bringing Windows 98 into line with the Windows NT business family. This is a basic Windows 95 module, since it helps you manage hard disks of more than 2 Gb capacity more efficiently and improve the overall performance of your PC.

However, the decision to switch to the FAT 32 format is not an easy one and you are advised to read the on-line help on this subject before you start the procedure. You should realize that some system utilities that work well with a FAT 16 facility may not operate any longer.

An irreversible conversion
If you choose to change to the 32-bit FAT mode, you will not be able to change back to 16-bit mode. Another consequence is that you will not be able to uninstall Windows 98 from this point forward and revert to Windows 95. Progress is forward; you cannot go backward.

Defragmenting a hard disk

By defragmenting your hard disk, you speed up subsequent processing. The aim is to store the data belonging to a particular file in a contiguous pattern. Any additions, modifications or deletions performed on all sorts of files (text, spreadsheet, database, etc.) generate pointers that provide a logical link between the data locations allocated to a given file. In effect, a particular file may have been created originally in an area of a given size and in the meantime that area may have been found to be too small to accommodate later additions. The additional data is stored in a vacant location away from the origional file. So, defragmentation consists in re-allocating adjacent spaces to various files.

The new defragmentation software keeps a record of the most frequently-used files and keeps a close eye on the files generated by the program. It actually positions those files close to their respective programs, thereby improving performance and speed.

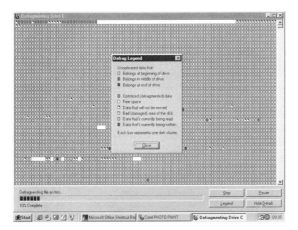

Figure 11.7: The defragmentation process, showing the types of sector in different colours and patterns

Backing-up files

The new backup facility recognizes SCSI tape drives and runs faster than that supplied with Windows 95.

The Backup Wizard guides you through the process step-by-step. You can back up the entire My Computer facility or specify the individual items to be backed up. To do this, simply check the boxes alongside the folders to back up. You can then decide to back up:

- selected files;
- new files; or
- modified files.

Checking the disk with Scandisk

Scandisk is one of the most frequently-used system tools. It checks the files (file allocation tables, or FAT) and the surface of the hard disk. If your PC shows signs of fatigue or responds oddly, run Scandisk straight away. Two checking methods are proposed:

- a standard check of files and folders;

- a more exacting check, which consists of analysing the disk surface (this can be quite a lengthy process, so you should run it when you do not need to use the PC).

You can ask Scandisk to correct errors automatically. The Advanced button allows you to configure individual settings:

- displaying a summary of the operations performed;

- using an overall log, keeping a record of all Scandisk actions. In some respects, this might be regarded as a bill of health for your PC;

- handling files with cross-links;

- converting fragments of lost files;

- checking file names.

Fig 11.8: The Scandisk settings

If you choose to analyse the disk surface, click Options to tell the software which areas to check. Scandisk can repair defective system or hidden files if you check this option.

Troubleshooting system files
Do not check System file repair until you have run the System file Troubleshooter. It should provide you with all the information you need if a major problem arises, and will attempt to carry out repairs by restoring any damaged files from the Windows 98 CD-ROM.

Figure 11.9: Analysing the surface of the hard disk

DriveSpace 3

DriveSpace 3 is a data-compression utility that enables you to double the capacity of your hard disk. If you compress drive C, DriveSpace 3 creates a compressed file, stored on logical disk F, for example. F is known as the *"host drive"*.

Disk F is not a compressed disk: it is a normal logical disk containing a compressed file.

Calling up the host drive
The host drive is shown in My Computer if it has a free capacity of at least 2 Mb. Drive C, the source disk, is always accessible, as well as the files it contains: however, it offers more free space.

DriveSpace 3 can be used to compress not the actual drive, but the free space on the disk. If your disk has 20 Mb of free space, you can switch to a capacity of 40 Mb.
To compress a disk, start the utility and select the drive to be compressed. In the Drive menu, choose Compress. The Decompress command performs the reverse operation.

When the drive has been compressed, you can adapt its characteristics in the Advanced Settings menu. You can set the amount of free space, change the compression ratio and alter the compression settings, depending on requirements.

You cannot compress a drive with DriveSpace 3 when its FAT has been changed to 32-bit mode (FAT converter).

The Compression Agent utility is used on a drive that has already been compressed to configure settings at file level. In this way, you adopt higher compression ratios for the least-used files.

ACTIVITY MONITORING TOOLS

There are two activity-monitoring tools:

- **the system monitor.** This monitors processor activity and resource usage.

- **the resource meter.** This utility works in the background, calculating usage of the system; of user resources; and of graphic display resources.

Hour 12

Windows 98 and multimedia applications

THE CONTENTS FOR THIS HOUR

- AutoPlay mode for CD-ROMs
- Multimedia accessories
- Multimedia plug-ins and players
- Audio and video on the Web
- Live radio on the Web
- The NetShow player
- Settings and monitoring
- Playing multimedia traffic on the Net
- Playing a DVD
- Image processing with Imaging

Compression is the multimedia spearhead on a PC. Without compression, just wave goodbye to the whole notion. For instance, by compressing music files, you can quarter file sizes whilst keeping a sound quality close to that of an audio CD. The process known as PCMCIA is most common, but it is an open architecture and Windows 98 can accept virtually any other compression technique. The compression methods employed do not result in any appreciable loss of quality. Only experienced music-lovers will detect the difference between two recordings, where one is compressed and the other is not.

Audio compression
Sound, like video, gobbles up disk space. For example, one second of CD-quality music requires about 170 kilobytes of storage space. To prevent your hard disk becoming full too quickly, you need to use sound compression algorithms. Windows 98 offers different compression tools. To this, you should add support for the MIDI standard (musical instrument digital interface).

Some audio compression tools are designed to process voice. This applies, in particular, to TrueSpeech, a process that allows you to compress voice signals and record them on the hard disk in real time. The TrueSpeech compression ratio is significant, because the frequency range used to reproduce faithfully the human voice is very narrow.

Whether for music or voice, compression opens up new horizons. Space-saving on the hard disk is not the only objective – far from it, because multimedia transmissions and networks have to be taken into account.

The MIDI standard for music
The MIDI standard is important for music files. Music scores enable us to describe a Beethoven sonata in just a few pages. But to play it, you need a quality piano and a talented interpreter. MIDI files resemble scores: they are control files that enable us to 'describe' music concisely. Windows 98 incorporates MIDI Polymessage, which handles MIDI files.

Windows 98 also incorporates all the resources needed to handle video in digital format (AVI – audiovideo interleave). Different compression methods (codecs) are available, including MPEG-oriented methods. This latter technology, which consumes vast decompression resources, normally requires the installation of a dedicated compression board.

In Windows 98, everything has been done to improve multimedia facilities and to assist their use. The AutoPlay mode (which appeared originally in Windows 95) is a typical example.

AUTOPLAY MODE FOR CD-ROMS

When you insert an audio compact disk in your hi-fi, the system automatically goes to the first track and plays the piece. So, why do we need to install a CD-ROM? And then, when it has been used once, why do we have to go back to the control to run it again?

With AutoPlay mode, when you insert a CD-ROM in your drive, Windows 98 checks whether an Autorun.inf file exists and, if so, the file is executed. Otherwise, Windows 98 carries out an automated installation procedure, creates the start-up file and runs it, without the need for you to do anything. The mere fact of inserting a disk means that you want to "play" it: so, Windows 98 takes over all the tasks which, until now, the user had to carry out.

MULTIMEDIA UTILITIES

Windows 98 is supplied with a number of multimedia utilities which you can call up from Start, Programs, Accessories, Entertainment.

The audio CD drive

Windows 98 allows you to use the CD-ROM drive to listen to audio CDs. The simple interface resembles the interface of a hi-fi system CD drive.

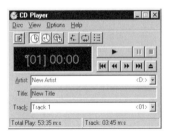

Figure 12.1: The audio CD drive

From the View menu, you can ask to display three additional areas:

- the toolbar;
- data on the disk and tracks; and
- the status bar.

The first icon on the left allows you to change the musical selection. The next three icons allow you to display, to the right of the track number, one of the following:

- the track time elapsed;
- the track time remaining; or
- the playing time remaining on the disk.

The other three icons are used to select:

- random play mode;
- uninterrupted listening; or
- listening to the introduction of each piece: each excerpt is played briefly, enabling you to go straight to a particular piece.

The intro listening time setting can be altered in the Options menu, under Preferences.

From the View menu, you can start-up the volume control utility, described below.

The sound recorder

The Windows 98 sound recorder reproduces the conventional interface of a real sound recorder, with the addition of a screen to display a graphic curve of the sound emitted.

Figure 12.2: The Windows 98 sound recorder

To record music or speech, you should first connect an audio source or a microphone to the sound board line input. Adjust the sound quality settings as required. To do this, click on Audio Properties in the Edit menu. The Audio Properties window then opens and you can set the recording conditions.

Then follow these steps:

1. From the File menu, click New to open a blank file.

2. Then click the record button (the sound recorder buttons imitate the conventions used by consumer electronics manufacturers).

3. Finally click on the black square to stop recording.

You can then check the recording as it plays.

In the File menu, you are invited to Record in, to save the sound file on the PC hard disk.

You can Increase or Decrease the volume, Adjust the echo, or even Invert sounds. These few features allow you to create all sorts of special sound effects.

You can only add an echo and invert the sound signal on an uncompressed file. The same applies to adjusting the volume level. You can modify the initial quality of a sound with the converter incorporated in the sound recorder. To do this, call up Properties from the File menu.

The sound recorder is a genuine mixing panel that also enables you to record a sound in a sound file. To do so, open a sound file and go to the position you want using the cursor and pressing Pause on play. Then start your recording. In this way, you can insert a sound file in another sound file or mix the sounds.

The multimedia player

The Windows 98 multimedia player can play sound files (WAV), video clips, animated images (AVI), musical sequences in MIDI format, or even play tracks on an audio CD (see Figure 12.3). Whatever type of multimedia file you load into the drive, you can use the "sound recorder" buttons to pause, stop, rewind or fast forward.

Figure 12.3: The multimedia player

When you play a video or animated sequence, an additional window opens, the size of which is set in the Video Properties window. You can alter the size again or switch to full-screen mode by clicking Properties in the multimedia player Peripherals menu. To hide the multimedia player window when viewing a clip, double-click in the player's title bar. To bring it up again, double-click in the title bar of the clip window.

Overall volume adjustment

The volume control can be called up directly or from a multimedia accessory. It can also be fetched from the right-hand side of the Taskbar. It allows you to adjust the volume for all the audio devices in your PC (see Figure 12.4). To alter the volume, slide the vertical bar. The horizontal cursor is used to set the balance between the loudspeakers.

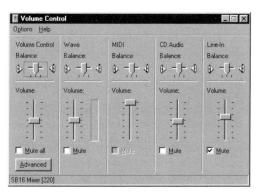

Figure 12.4: Adjusting the volume of audio devices

The volume and balance controls affect WAV files, MIDI files, the audio CD, the line input and even your microphone or loudspeakers. From Properties in the Options menu, you can check the devices to be displayed and call up the volume control for playback, recording, or voice commands.

PLUG-INS AND PLAYERS

With the help of software search and compression techniques, the multimedia phenomenon has surfaced on the Web, to the point where we now talk of Web channels, rather than Web sites. Of course, marketing accounts for much of this, but we should not ignore the facts: computer animation, audio and video have had a profound effect on the Web.

Even with our good old telephone line on the Public Switched Telephone Network (PSTN), we can benefit from the wealth of multimedia facilities offered by the Web. To do this, you need two sorts of tool:

- plug-ins; and
- players.

These names conceal very simple concepts. A plug-in is a small program that is placed in the browser in order to run certain features, such as executing a computer animation. This is what is done by Real Audio and Real Video from Progressive Networks.

A player is a stand-alone software package responsible for meeting requirements that the browser cannot offer as standard, such as playing audio or video files available on the Web. NetShow, designed by Microsoft, is one example. Files in NetShow format are not yet as common as the Real Audio and Real Video formats, but you can be sure that Microsoft will push forward the technology.

Figure 12.5: Listening to Real Audio files continuously on the Web

NetShow is thus used to exploit the multimedia sources found on the Web. Of course, other technologies are available and, to make the most of them, you should from time to time load the plug-ins which have been incorporated in the Internet Explorer 4.0 browser.

AUDIO AND VIDEO

Audio and video are new features on the Web, but the bandwidth of the telephone network does not allow you at present to display video in real time in optimum conditions with the result that playing video is slow and image quality is poor. You have to settle for smaller documents with image refresh once a second at best. While we know that video is generally full-screen at a rate of twenty five frames per second, we are still some way off achieving this.

Consequently, on the Web, audio is overtaking video because it requires fewer resources. We should distinguish between two sorts of audio-video application:

- **off-line.** The files are downloaded to the PC and then played locally.

- **in real time, or "live".** The sources are played back directly from the Web, without storing them in the PC.

Whilst real time video at present is something of a misnomer, real time audio – radio, in effect – works perfectly well.

Listening to the radio on the Web
For this you need a quality modem connection:at least 28.8 kbps and a PC with a good configuration. Needless to say, microwave radio stations have seized upon this technology. Today, hundreds of radio stations throughout the world offer "live" listening from their transmitters. Whilst direct hi-fi broadcasting has not yet arrived, it is still possible to download audio programmes using high fidelity technology.

THE NETSHOW PLAYER

With Microsoft NetShow 2.0, you can make the most of the multimedia traffic supplied on the Internet, or through your corporate intranet. Generally, the NetShow player is loaded in your PC when Windows 98 is installed. If not, you can use the add-programs module from the Control Panel and use the Windows 98 component installation dialog box. You can also visit the Microsoft site to download the latest version of the software or obtain additional components (compression, for example).

The NetShow technology is designed to handle continuous multimedia traffic: it therefore applies to computer animations (2D, synthesised animations), to audio and to video. There is no need any longer for you to download a video, as it is played live under the best possible conditions: sometimes, too, under the worst conditions, if the network is congested or your modem is too slow. NetShow is a Microsoft product, but open to the compression technologies of other publishers. These are what are called codecs in multi media jargon

Hence, NetShow uses a dedicated format, known as ASF *(Active Stream Format)*. The technology operates in unicast or multicast mode. In unicast mode, the Web server sends a single data stream that can be controlled by the user as if it were a conventional video. You can also use the fast-forward, rewind and stop buttons to handle the video traffic. This can be quite punishing in terms of bandwidth, since each user can make specific demands on a particular stream and generate as many streams as he does requests. In multicast mode, a single copy of the video data stream is sent to users who request it. This is a bit like watching television: you see the content, but you cannot go back or speed up the programme. This is the most commonly-used broadcasting method.

Running NetShow

There are three ways of running NetShow:

- directly from Start;

- directly from a link in a Web page; or

- indirectly from a Web page: the player is embedded in a Visual Basic script or an ActiveX control (also widely known as an *applet*).

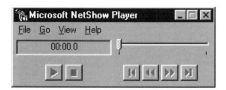

Figure 12.6: Running NetShow from the Start menu (Programs, Internet Explorer)

You can open an ASF file in two ways:

- from the PC hard disk: the Open file command in the File menu.

- on the Internet: the Open site command; here you enter the full URL that leads to the file in question (**http://www.server.file.asf**).

Handling the operating settings

To obtain the operating properties in NetShow, click the View menu and go to Play settings.

The Advanced dialog box shows the broadcasting protocol used and allows you to adjust the size of the buffer memory. This represents the volume of ASF data that the software stores in advance. Once the buffer is full, the software reads the data and at the same time stores fresh ASF data.

Figure 12.7: The Advanced play settings

The compression systems, or codecs, used by the software can also be accessed from the Properties window. To do this, click the Codecs tab. Generally speaking, the codecs convert a compressed format to another format which is not compressed. The advantage of these tools is that they cut disk storage requirements and reduce the amount of bandwidth needed.

As a general rule, you need not concern yourself with the codecs. Just be aware that different compression/decompression methods exist on the market and you will be expected to adopt new methods when you download, to suit your particular needs.

The properties of an ASF data stream can be checked on the Details tab in Properties.

This provides the following information:

- the file path to the continuously broadcast ASF file;

- the creation date;

- the duration, except for live shows;

- the ideal bandwidth: this is the value specified when the ASF file was created;

- the error-correction method; and

- the picture dimensions.

The broadcasting statistics can be looked up from the Statistics dialog box.

Figure 12.8: Statistics on multimedia data stream broadcasting

Playing "unicast" traffic
Before you can view a video, for example, your connection must be set up to the data stream. The buffer is then loaded and playing begins. At this point, you can take up position on markers, if the program contains any, or you can use sound recorder type functions in unicast mode.

The ActiveMovie technology
ActiveMovie is another video-playing technology supplied with Windows 98. To open an ActiveMovie control, click Start, select Programs, then Accessories and Multimedia.

PLAYING DVD DISKS

Windows 98 comes ready to cater for the new generation of very high capacity disks, in this case the DVD *(Digital Versatile Disk)*. This allows you to show sophisticated films and multimedia programmes on your PC.

DVD drives use USB or IEEE 1394 type connections. Once the drive has been fitted in your PC, you should configure the settings or make Windows 98 recognize it automatically (Add New Hardware procedure on the Control Panel).

Finally, you need to install the DVD player supplied with Windows 98. To do this, go to the Control Panel again, click Add/Delete programs and then select the Windows Installation tab. In the Multimedia window, check the DVD Player box and start the installation process from the Windows 98 CD-ROM.

Hi-fi on your PC
The tools required to play a CD-ROM (or audio CD), the volume control, or the multimedia clip player – already familiar from Windows 95 – can be called up in the Entertainment menu in the Accessories folder (through Start and Programs). This is also where you access the DVD player software.

IMAGE PROCESSING WITH IMAGING

We got to know the Microsoft Paint software which evolved slowly through the various versions of Windows. It is still available in Windows 98, but is now challenged by Imaging for Windows, a program designed by Kodak.

Being comprehensive and more powerful, it incorporates a colour management module, document digitizing settings (Tools menu), the ability to store documents in a format adapted for sending images by fax, and quick annotation functions (Annotation menu).

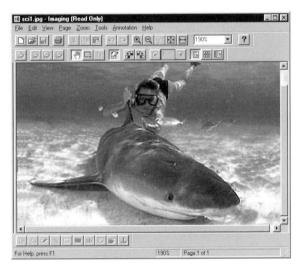

Figure 12.9: Image processing with Imaging

Index

F

G

H

I

Windows 98

S

Scandisk 27, 179, 185
Scheduled tasks 34, 176
Scheduling set-up routines 25
Screensaver 73
Find (command) 42, 100,
    the Internet 100
    the Web 147
Search engines 101, 147
Security areas 136
Security certificates 136
Sending and Receiving 160
Server
    mail 129
    news 129
Server type 124
Settings
    for the joystick 76
    for the keyboard 71
    for the modem 85
    for the PC 25
    for volumes 195
    for Windows 179
Shortcuts 32, 59, 65, 66
Single click 76
Software
    drawing 92
    Internet mail 8
    Internet browser 9
Sorting messages 164
Standard buttons 61
Start button 33, 39, 59, 98

creating a shortcut 66
customisation 67
settings 50
Starting a program 59
Starting up
    the browser 103, 137
    the Internet connection 141
    Outlook Express 103
    Windows Explorer 62
Start menu 98
Stop (command) 47
Storing in Favorites 148
Subscription to a Web channel 131
Subscription to a site 151
Subscriptions 152
Switchboard 102
Switching from one task to another 54
System file troubleshooter 179, 181
System information 179, 180
System tasks
    programming scheduler 176

T

Taskbar 32, 39, 55, 103
    settings 49
TCP/IP 9, 124, 125, 126
Text label 62
Tidying up the hard disk 179, 182

212